The Art of
GIVING
QUALITY
SERVICE

Mary Gober

Mary Gober International
Clarence, New York

The Art of Giving Quality Service

Copyright 1984, 2004 by Mary Gober
Mary Gober International

Published by
Mary Gober International

Distributed by
Mary Gober International
P. O. Box 407
Clarence, New York   14031

Email marygober@marygober.com
Telephone +1 716 759 2847
Facsimile +1 716 759 8165

Website www.marygober.com

Twenty-Second Printing, May 2004

ISBN 0-9624563-0-6

DEDICATED

To **you** and all Service-Givers,
the world over,
who enjoy helping others!

ACKNOWLEDGMENTS

To my many clients and a number of people who have made a special contribution to me and the success of this book.

A BIG "Thank You" to -

- Jane Burke, my Executive Assistant, for always taking personal responsibility for all the details and giving me ... Peace of Mind

- Daniel Joyce, Hirsch & Joyce, for your expertise and astute counsel

and

- Dolores and Robert Gober, my parents, my Mainstay ...

Contents

PREFACE

During the past 24 years, I have traveled over two million miles, visiting and presenting seminars in over 24 countries around the world. In the course of my travels, I have used commercial and charter airlines, trains, boats, buses, rental cars, private cars, limousines and taxis. I've eaten in hundreds of restaurants and stayed in countless hotels and motels in a wide variety of countries and cities.

During these travels, I have encountered all kinds of service. In addition, in my private life, I have experienced the normal service transactions involving banks, hospitals, insurance companies, travel agencies, libraries, beauty salons, local, state and federal government agencies, telephone companies, utilities, retail stores of all kinds, appliance service companies, auto agencies, real estate agencies, income tax services, moving companies, recreational facilities, volunteer organizations, professional associations, manufacturer's service departments and professionals such as lawyers, dentists, doctors, architects, etc.

Some organizations and service-givers gave me wonderful service. The transactions were quick, competent, courteous and effective. I was pleased and enjoyed telling the service-givers involved of my satisfaction. The service-givers were obviously good at their jobs, enjoyed helping others and represented their organizations extremely well. Although these high-quality service transactions tended to be rare, I have continued to patronize these quality service organizations as often as I can.

In some situations, however, the service I was given was terrible, and I ended up frustrated, angry and resentful. Sometimes this was because service-givers simply did not know their jobs, though they were courteous and empathetic. In other cases, although the service-givers were technically competent, I was met with rude, uncaring, indifferent behavior. Regardless of the cause, I, of course, have carefully tried to avoid having anything further to do with these service-givers and their organizations.

If the service was bad, I complained. Again I noticed big differences in how my complaints were handled. Some organizations seemed to accept complaints easily, and I was handled with empathy, courtesy and prompt consideration. In other cases my complaints were avoided or met with hostility, dishonesty and time-wasting run-arounds. Fortunately, those situations where service was really bad and my complaints were handled poorly were rare.

The vast majority of service transactions I have experienced and observed tended to be characterized by a kind of mediocrity. The service-givers seemed bored or frustrated and were obviously not enjoying their jobs, although they did manage to get things done. Those customers who received the service seemed not to enjoy the transaction at all and appeared grateful just to complete the exchange with no major problems arising.

The more I thought about the different quality levels of service-giving, the more I became interested in these questions: "Why the differences? What is it that seems to lead to high quality service, and what makes for poor service? Why is so much service-giving mediocre and satisfying to neither the customer or the service-giver?"

Since I was in the business of helping organizations train their Supervisors, Managers, Salespeople and Secretaries to become more effective in their jobs, I began to study service-giving jobs. I wondered, "Could service-givers be taught ideas and techniques that would help them deliver quality service? Could they learn skills that would reduce their job stress and help them enjoy their jobs more?"

I began to more carefully observe service-givers of all kinds. I was determined to find out what attitudes, ideas and skills superior service-givers seemed to possess. I also wanted to find out what poor quality service-givers seemed to lack in their approach to their jobs.

I quickly became convinced there was a set of attitudes and skills that could be taught to service-givers. I felt these could help them learn how to deliver quality service and to satisfy their clients and customers. I was certain these techniques could also help their organizations and reduce job frustration and stress for service-givers.

My first chance to put my ideas into practice came in Saudi Arabia. In 1980, The Arabian American Oil Company, ARAMCO, asked me to develop training programs for a multi-cultural mix of service-givers. I was assigned to work with a wide variety of service-giving jobs involved in their company community. These included hotel personnel, telephone operators and repairmen, receptionists, housing and restaurant employees, recreational staff, postal and retail operations, doctors, nurses, medical technicians and maintenance and repair service center technicians.

First I looked carefully at the work being performed. I quickly discovered there were skills in dealing with people that applied to all jobs. Next I conducted several pilot training programs with participants drawn from different service-giving jobs. To my delight, the pilot programs proved successful. Following the training, there were immediate improvements in the quality of service being given. I became convinced the attitudes and skills I taught were sound and worked well when put into practice in real service-giving situations.

Following the pilot programs, I trained other instructors within the company and translated my Quality Service course into Arabic. My Quality Service courses were presented to several thousand employees and in all cases, I got the same successful results. I learned that when service-givers put into practice the principles they were taught, both the quality of service and their job satisfaction improved, often dramatically.

From that experience I went on to present my Quality Service course to other organizations outside Saudi Arabia. In some cities I have done public training programs where service-givers who attended came from many different types of organizations. I have continued to get the same successful results. Quality service skills are universal and can be utilized by service-givers from a wide variety of organizations and different countries.

As I have worked with more and more organizations, I have frequently been asked for some sort of publication summarizing the essential ideas contained in my Quality Service course. This book is in response to that request.

I realized there are countless names for service-giving jobs: teller, ticket agent, nurse, receptionist, doctor, beautician, clerk, reservationist, flight attendant, field service representative, salesperson, serviceman, etc. Because of this I decided I had to find one term to use in this book to describe anyone whose job involved giving service.

I decided on the term "service-giver." You may not have ever used this term to describe what you do. But it serves to identify the common nature of hundreds of different kinds of jobs in different sectors of our economy, the purpose of which is giving service to others.

Throughout this book I have also used another term, "customer," to refer to the people to whom you give service. You may be more familiar with terms like patient, patron, client, passenger or guest. However, for simplicity sake and ease of reading, I selected the one term, customer, to identify those you serve.

I feel strongly that service organizations and their employees will find this book useful in helping them put into practice the essential attitudes and skills of quality service. By improving the quality of their service, organizations will obviously benefit. So will their customers.

But I hope you, the service-giver, will gain the major benefits. I hope that you will discover that by using the quality service techniques outlined in this book, you will find your job much more enjoyable and satisfying and less frustrating and stressful. I hope you will hear, more often, the heartfelt thanks and appreciation of your satisfied customers.

I know I would benefit from learning from you, too. If you have any experiences, service ideas or feedback on this book that you would like to share, I'd love to hear from you.

I wish you the best of luck!

Mary S. Gober

1. You Make the Difference

Stella Wilson is a teller at First National Bank. As a service-giver, she tries hard to keep her customers happy. After work yesterday she went to her dentist, Dr. Ed Brown.

Ed Brown enjoys working with his patients, and after taking care of Stella, he went down to his local library to pick up some travel books for a trip he was planning to take with his family.

Frieda Clark, the librarian, welcomed Dr. Brown as one of her regular patrons and helped him find just what he wanted.

That evening, Frieda went to the airport to fly to St. Louis so she could attend her sister's wedding.

On the plane, Sheila McGraw, a flight attendant, served Frieda and her other passengers their dinners quickly and efficiently.

That night, Sheila checked in at a hotel near the airport where she was to lay over before flying out again the next day.

Carl Rodriguez, the hotel registration desk clerk, welcomed Sheila with a friendly greeting and recognized her as a frequent guest at the hotel.

The next day, Carl went to see his lawyer about making out a will. Bill Chan, his lawyer, was happy to see his client Carl again and was able to make several, helpful suggestions which Carl appreciated.

Every day millions of such service transactions take place. Today we live in a service economy with over 50 million people employed in some kind of service-giving job. In the future it is expected that jobs in farming, mining and manufacturing will continue to disappear, and even more of us will be engaged in some sort of service-giving occupation.

That's why you, as a service-giver, are so important in today's economy. And whether you call them patients, guests, clients, patrons, passengers or customers, people count on you for help.

As our service economy has grown, so has the competition between organizations. But many organizations offer almost the exact same service. You can buy the same at several different automobile dealers in your community. Different airlines will fly you to the same destination, often at the same cost. Banks offer you the same savings and checking account services, frequently at identical rates of interest. Repair services charge the same hourly rate and you have several to choose from in getting an appliance repaired. Restaurants offer similar menus, often at about the same cost.

But one thing can never be the same in different organizations. The people. That's why you, as a service-giver, are so critical to your organization's success. You make the difference. Your job skills, attitudes and abilities to handle people help distinguish your organization from others who offer similar services. In many cases, YOU are the only competitive edge your organization has!

In most organizations, you as a service-giver are the only contact customers have with your organization. Take a rental car agency, for instance. For the customer, if you are the person behind the desk helping them obtain a car, **you** are the organization. And how you look, what you say and do, is what will create a lasting impression on the customer.

If the service is bad, the whole organization will be discounted. The customer may decide never to do business with that organization again...even in other locations thousands of miles away!

If the service is high quality, customers may decide regardless of where they go, they will continue to use the services of that car rental agency.

It's that simple. You, as a service-giver, can make or break your organization. And it's true of every type of service organization.

All service-givers have one thing in common. Even though their job as nurse, librarian, retail store clerk, delivery person, receptionist, telephone operator, travel agent, recreation director, taxi driver, ticket agent or tax accountant may differ technically, they all deal with people.

Chances are you know the technical side of your job pretty well. If you don't, you probably are learning it. But most service-givers realize to **really** improve their ability to serve others, they need to improve their skills in handling people.

That's why this book will be helpful to you. It will show you more effective ways you can handle your customers. And it explains how you can avoid problems and improve the satisfaction of the people you serve. It will also help you do your part in increasing your organization's ability to compete in today's service economy.

But what's in it for you? Why try hard to improve your performance as a service-giver by learning better people-handling skills? Let's look at just a few of the benefits you can enjoy from using these quality service techniques.

First of all, you'll enjoy your job more. Instead of frowns, hostile stares and gripes from your customers, you'll be on the receiving end of smiles, compliments and expressions of appreciation and gratitude.

The frustrations and stress of helping others, usually working against an impossible workload and unreal time demands, will be reduced. You'll find that using quality service techniques will allow you to remain calm, relaxed and polite. It will help you avoid time-wasting mistakes and errors, and your calm and courteous manner will become contagious. You'll find that customers will become more reasonable and less demanding because you will be giving them service that is quick and efficient.

As job stress is reduced, you'll enjoy the benefits of better eating and sleeping and your health will improve. You may also discover that with reduced job stress, personal and family relationships will become more satisfying.

You'll also find that cooperation from fellow service-givers is improved. Less tension and hostility will occur between you and the other service-givers on whom you depend for help. Quality service-giving calls for teamwork. Instead of fighting both customers **and** fellow-service-givers, you'll find you are fighting neither!

With the use of quality service skills and attitudes, your relationship with your manager will also improve. There will be less need to involve your manager in mistakes and problems, less need to give them "bad news" and less need to have to explain and defend yourself in the face of criticism. As compliments and congratulations from your customers increase, you'll be getting praise and appreciation from your manager, too.

And with a better relationship with your manager, come better chances for career advancement. As you show you can really handle your job as a service-giver well, you will be demonstrating your readiness for a position of higher authority and responsibility in the organization.

Even within your present job, you'll find that by using quality service skills you'll more than likely be given more responsibility and authority.

You'll also get the satisfaction that comes with knowing you are a true "professional," not only handling the technical side of your job well, but being a "pro" at handling people, too.

And don't forget, you are also a "service-receiver." As you develop your service-giving skills, you'll discover you are a more discriminating, efficient customer as well!

But perhaps most of all you'll enjoy the deep, personal satisfaction that comes with knowing you have helped others correctly, completely and to the best of your ability. You'll enjoy knowing even though you are not always able to give customers everything they want, the way you work with them will leave them fully satisfied with your professional efforts.

You Make the Difference

There are 50 million service-givers in the United States today. Competition between service organizations that offer similar services has increased. Frequently the only difference between these organizations is the performance of their employees. Customers often evaluate an entire organization based on one transaction with a single service-giver.

Although service-giving jobs may differ from one another in a technical way, they all have one thing in common, dealing with people.

By learning the basic skills of quality service-giving presented in this book, you will:

* Enjoy your job more
* Reduce job stress
* Improve your health and personal relationships
* Take pride in being a professional
* Become a better "service-receiver"
* Take pleasure in the satisfaction of helping others
* Prepare yourself for career advancement

2. What Do Customers Really Want?

Why do customers do the things they do? What turns them on? What turns them off? Why are they sometimes happy? Why are they sometimes angry? What do customers want in a service transaction?

The answers to these questions are not easy. Psychologists have been working on them for years. But as a service-giver, your success depends on handling people properly. You need to know the 12 basic needs that motivate customers and make them do the things they do.

1. Control

Customers need to feel they are in control of the situation. They need to feel they can make things come out their way and they are not being taken advantage of, manipulated or deceived.

Sandy Dempsey was planning her vacation and was trying to select a tour with her travel agent. The agent didn't seem to be giving Sandy all the alternatives available to help her make a good decision. Sandy felt as though she was being manipulated and steered toward the tour the travel agent wanted her to have, rather than being allowed to make her own choice. This made her feel very uncomfortable. She decided to take her business elsewhere and left the travel agency.

2. Goals

Customers need to feel that whatever they are doing is helping them move toward their goals. Most of the things we do in life are in pursuit of some goal. We are constantly seeking those things that are important to us, things we feel will bring us happiness and satisfaction.

Michael and Linda were a young couple trying to furnish their new house. They were buying expensive furniture because they wanted to establish a nice home that reflected their taste. They appreciated reassurance that the furniture they were buying would help them meet that goal.

6

3. Self-image

Customers like to feel good about themselves as they go about their daily lives. They like to think of themselves as doing the right thing, that they are intelligent and competent, not foolish or silly. They like to interact with those who help them maintain their positive image of themselves.

Clayton Wilson was a plumber repairing the hot water heating system in the Wellington's home. After he was finished, he explained the proper operation of the system to avoid future maintenance problems. He reassured the Wellingtons they themselves could make minor adjustments and do minor maintenance on the system if they wanted to. He avoided making them feel foolish or guilty about neglecting the system. They enjoyed Clayton's visit and assured him they would call him in the future if they needed repair services again.

4. Fairness

One of a customer's strongest drives involves a sense of fairness. They like to feel that in any service transaction, they are being treated fairly and appropriately when compared to others.

Michele Ward was a businesswoman traveling alone. In her hotel dining room she was seated and left waiting. She noticed others who came in after she did were waited on promptly. She was very angry about what she considered unfair treatment and complained to the headwaiter.

5. Friendliness

Customers want to feel good about those with whom they interact. They want to trust them and have confidence in them. They like service-givers to be friendly and warm so they, as customers, can enjoy a pleasant service transaction.

Joanne Simpson was a bank teller. She never smiled, never looked at her customers and never used their names. She was always businesslike, but cold and impersonal. Customers waiting in line tried to avoid her window. They preferred to do business with the other tellers who greeted them by name, smiled and made the transaction pleasant and enjoyable.

6. Understanding

Customers always want to know WHAT is happening and why, so they can understand what's going on around them. In service-giving situations they get frustrated and angry when they are unable to get the information they want. They don't like it when things are not explained to them so they can really understand what's going on.

Wendy Johnson took her car in for servicing after she heard strange noises in the engine. The service-writer used a lot of technical terms and confused her with his explanations. She left the car, but felt miserable and afraid the repairs would be too costly because she didn't really understand what was going to be done or why.

7. Security

Customers have a strong need to feel safe and secure. They like predictable situations where they are familiar with everything and know what's going to happen. That's why they often hesitate to change services or products, or move to a new city. In service situations they get apprehensive when they think their safety or security is threatened.

Tom Tracy took his family to a new recreation park that had just opened up. But as soon as he got there, he felt uneasy. Things were so noisy and confused he couldn't figure out where to go or what to do. The rides didn't look as though they were safe and everything was dirty and messy. He decided to leave because he didn't feel this was a place he and his family could enjoy.

8. Approval and Recognition

Customers like to have the approval and acceptance of others. Praise and recognition by others is one of their most powerful motivators. From our first efforts as babies to gain the approval of our parents, we all spend a lot of time trying to get others to recognize us for our accomplishments.

When Harry Dunbar was given the Clubman-of-the-Year Award by his organization, he was pleased and proud. That night, to his surprise, he found a congratulatory fruit basket in his room from the hotel management where the award banquet had been held. He felt proud and pleased that the hotel had taken time to acknowledge his accomplishment and made a mental note to use the hotel in the future for his own company's meetings.

9. Importance

All customers like to feel they are important and essential. In service-giving situations, they want service-givers to recognize their importance and not ignore them or treat them as unimportant. They like prompt, full attention and to have their time and activities given the proper consideration.

Ruby Mason was a manager in a small company. She arrived at her doctor's office at her appointed time, 2:00 p.m. At 3:30 she still hadn't seen the doctor, and the nurse failed to keep her informed of any reasons for the delay. Ruby left feeling insulted and frustrated and resolved to change doctors since this had happened before.

10. Appreciation

Customers like to feel appreciated. Especially if they invest a large amount of time, energy or money in something. They want that effort to be appreciated by those who benefit from it. In dealing with organizations they patronize, customers like to know their business is valued and appreciated, especially if they are regular customers.

Rick Manner was a hard-working manufacturer's representative. Three times a week he traveled on the same airline to make calls in different cities. He saw the same airline desk personnel on almost all his trips, even the same flight attendants. None of the airline service-givers ever told him they appreciated his business, even though he spent thousands of dollars each month with that airline.

11. Belonging

Customers like to identify with organizations. They belong to clubs, neighborhood groups and volunteer organizations. They like to feel they contribute to others, and that others contribute to them as members of the same group. They enjoy being identified as people who belong to a group. In service-giving situations, customers are often proud of their affiliation with an organization. They like the feeling of being a regular customer and "belonging" to that organization. Service-givers who recognize regular customers, greet them by name and acknowledge their affiliation, help their customers satisfy that sense of belonging.

Fred and Alice Caruthers and Joe and Jackie Taylor had been taking their vacation together at the same resort for nearly 15 years. They were always greeted warmly by the owners and given special attention. When the owners introduced new staff members to the Taylors and Caruthers, they were always told, "Take good care of these people, they're part of the family here!"

12. Honesty

Customers have a strong need to feel they can trust and have confidence in service-givers and their organizations. This is especially true today because so many customers have been the victims of false advertising, broken promises and poor service.

Bob Andrews was a manufacturing plant manager. His plant was having all kinds of problems with a piece of equipment they had recently purchased from the Ajax Company. When he called the Ajax Company's service department, one of their field representatives advised him that the problem must be with Bob's own maintenance procedures as the Ajax equipment had had no problems of this kind before. Later, Bob happened to be at a trade show and met several other manufacturing people who told him they had similar problems with their Ajax equipment. That kind of dishonesty made Bob angry, and he decided that he wouldn't buy anything else from Ajax again.

Determining Customer's Needs

These 12 needs apply to customers in general. To really use this information to good advantage, you need to be able to determine which needs are most important to a particular customer in a given situation. There are three techniques you can use to do this.

Ask Questions

By asking your customers, you can help determine what their primary needs are at the time you are working with them.

Listen

By listening carefully to what your customers say and how they say it, you can also help determine what their needs are. And don't just listen to the words, try to listen for the feelings behind the words. Pay close attention to what they are telling you, what they ask about, what they comment on. Use these clues to zero in on the need they seem to be trying to satisfy.

Observe

Watch how your customers are acting. Pay particular attention to their facial expressions and posture. Notice what they might be carrying, how they are dressed, who they have with them, etc. By being alert and observing your customers you can sometimes pick up valuable clues that will help you determine their needs.

In the rest of this book you'll learn more about these specific skills and how to use them in interacting with customers. Keep in mind that quality service-givers ask themselves, "What does this customer seem to need and want from me? Can I satisfy that need as I take care of them?"

By thinking this way, you can improve the service you give your customers and make the transaction a more satisfying one for both of you.

What Do Customers Really Want?

Your success as a service-giver depends on how well you handle customers. Understanding what your customers need and want is essential to quality service-giving. Customers in general have 12 basic needs:.

* Control
* Goals
* Self-Image
* Fairness
* Friendliness
* Understanding
* Security
* Approval and Recognition
* Importance
* Appreciation
* Belonging
* Honesty

To determine the particular needs of an individual customer in a given situation, you need to:

* Ask Questions
* Listen
* Observe

3. What Do Quality Service-Givers Do?

What are "quality" service-givers? What do they do? How do they think and feel? These were the questions I tried to answer in my research with thousands of different service-givers. My interviews and observations took place in hundreds of different service agencies, insurance companies, hospitals, hotels, restaurants, airlines, car rental agencies, professional offices, customer service departments, appliance service companies, retail stores, moving companies, recreational facilities, government agencies, libraries, utilities, real estate agencies, employment agencies, volunteer and professional organizations, and many others as well.

In all these organizations I found that service-givers differed in their attitudes, knowledge and skills. And these differences affected their performance. Many seemed to do just a mediocre job. A few did a poor job, and a few did an excellent job of consistently giving their clients and customers superior service.

I concentrated on these superior service-givers. I called them "quality" service-givers and have identified the qualities and characteristics which set them apart and made them superior performers. These descriptive characteristics seemed to fall into two categories: (1) service-givers and their customers, which I have subdivided into four parts, and (2) service-givers and their own organization.

As a service-giver you can use this as a checklist. Compare your performance with this list. How do you measure up? Chances are you'll find at least a few areas where you feel you could improve.

I Service-Givers and Their Customers

A. Attitudes Toward Customers

1. Enjoy Helping People

This is what service-giving is really all about, helping people meet their needs and solve their problems. Quality service-givers enjoy doing that. They see problems as opportunities for being of service to others. Customers quickly respond to this type of service-giver since it is easy for them to recognize such service-givers as ready, able and eager to serve them.

2. Handle People Well

In addition to knowing the technical parts of their job well, quality service-givers also know how to handle people. They consider this part of their job just as important as the technical side, and maybe even more so. They understand that sometimes customers are just as much interested in HOW things were done for them, as they are in WHAT was done. That's why quality service-givers are empathetic. They are sensitive to the needs and wants of other people and know how to handle people in a wide variety of situations.

3. Care for Their Customers

Watching out for their customers' safety and welfare is one of the things effective service-givers do best. They make sure the areas where customers are going to visit are clean, safe and comfortable. And they keep an eye out for ANYTHING that will make it more convenient for their customers to do business with them. Good service-givers make sure every part of the service transaction is set up not just for the organization's convenience, but for the customer's convenience, as well.

4. Give Fair and Equal Treatment to All

Quality service-givers give the same attention, care and concern to all of their customers regardless of age, race, religion or ethnic background. They make sure everyone they deal with is treated fairly.

14

5. Never Use Their Job Authority to "Punish" People

Service-givers, often frustrated and under stress, may sometimes be tempted to use their job authority to "punish" those who have been giving them a hard time. Quality service-givers never do this. They realize they may have certain power to make life miserable for customers, to make them wait, to make them come back the next day at great inconvenience, etc. But effective service-givers resist that temptation, they play it straight and take no pleasure in "getting even."

B. Skills In Dealing With Customers

1. Know the Technical Parts of Their job

Every job requires certain technical knowledge and skills. Good service-givers know their job. They are competent and able to do all parts of their job, and do them well. They pride themselves on their effectiveness and their efficiency in knowing what to do, when and how. And if they are given new things to learn, they learn them quickly so as to maintain their high standards of efficiency.

2. Follow a Consistent Method for Giving Service

Later in this book you'll find the 7-step method of giving good service. Most quality service-givers follow these seven steps in *every* transaction. They realize that by using this method they can continue to offer their customers quality service, day in and day out, not just once in a while. Using the method gives them confidence to handle any service transaction.

3. Reassure People About Their Service

Most customers have had bad service experiences. In some cases they may approach a service-giver with a chip on their shoulder, expecting to be badly treated and ready to fight. That's why quality service-givers take time to reassure their customers they are going to be given the best possible service. This frequently helps avoid misunderstandings or problems before they arise.

4. Communicate Effectively

All quality service transactions are based on good communications: listening, talking, writing or reading. Quality service-givers have learned how to read carefully and accurately, write clearly and use good handwriting or keyboarding skills. They are able to make themselves understood by speaking clearly, loudly enough and slowly enough, and using language and terminology that customers can easily understand. Quality service-givers also listen well. They pay close attention when listening to others and don't interrupt. They understand communicating, though it seems simple, is full of possible misunderstandings that can be harmful to all concerned. So, they are always careful to communicate effectively, whether listening, talking, writing or reading.

5. Refer People When Necessary

When they are unable to help their clients or customers, effective service-givers know where to send people for help. They know other people in their organization who might be able to help, or in some cases, they refer their customers to other organizations that might help them. But they do this only when they are quite sure they are unable to give their customers what they want.

Lisa Tyler was a bank teller. When she couldn't help her customer with a question involving a complicated transfer of funds internationally, she referred him to the bank's International Department, giving her customer the name of the person to ask for and exact instructions on how to get to their office.

6. Always Use Courtesy

One of the most distinguishing features of quality service-givers is they are always friendly and polite to their customers. They use courtesy words and phrases and demonstrate courteous behavior. They continue to be polite and friendly even in a tough situation where they have to deal with an irate customer.

Jose Chanos had been working a long shift at the front desk of his hotel. A big convention in town had made reservations tight everywhere. When a customer came in and was told his reservation wasn't in the records, the customer blew his top. He started to shout and slam the desk. Jose said, "I'm really sorry that you are upset, and I can understand why. If you'll please let me help you, I will try to find you other accommodations at another hotel." His calm, polite offering of help caused the customer to cool down right away.

Quality service-givers are also courteous to their fellow employees, realizing courtesy is contagious. They understand an important part of good human relations: most people, when they see others being polite and friendly, tend to act the same way themselves.

7. Are Neat, Clean, and Well-Organized

Quality service-givers can often be identified by just looking at them. They keep themselves neat and clean and always look sharp. They keep their clothing or uniforms clean and neat as well, and are always dressed appropriately for the job. Their concern with cleanliness and neatness extends to their workplace, and they make sure the areas where they work are clean, neat and well-organized. They follow the rule, "A place for everything, and everything in its place."

8. Use the Telephone Effectively

Because more and more service is being handled by phone, quality service-givers have developed their telephone skills. They know the special problems of communicating by telephone and how to handle them. They also know the ins and outs of telephone management and the proper way of taking and leaving messages.

9. Use Their Time Well

Knowing how much time to take is a critical skill that effective service-givers have developed. They know customers don't want to be dealt with too quickly. But they also know customers don't want to waste time and be delayed unnecessarily. Taking the right amount of time to help and responding quickly to customers are the two important skills here.

10. Help Educate Customers

Effective service-givers realize they can help themselves by helping educate their customers. This can mean a simple explanation of a form, or procedure so the next time the customer's transaction is speeded up or made easier. Or it can mean watching for what customers do that is correct and helpful in the service transaction, and then commenting on that, reinforcing or rewarding the customer for having the right forms ready, or providing the right information ahead of time, etc. This makes the service transaction easier for all concerned.

Larry Taylor is a dentist. For all his new patients he prepared a booklet explaining office procedures, insurance and billing and how appointments were to be handled. It also included information on his approach to dental care. On the first appointment, he went over the booklet with his patient. This avoided a lot of potential problems later on and made it easier for his patients to use his services.

C. Preventing Customer Dissatisfaction

1. Anticipate Customer Needs

Because of their experience on the job, quality service-givers often can anticipate what customers need, sometimes even before the customers are aware of those needs themselves. Effective service-givers anticipate these needs and are quick to offer customers help beyond what they ask for.

Claudia Eastman was an interior decorator for a large furniture store. She had worked with the Greensmiths before in helping them decorate their home. She knew they wanted an overall, integrated theme in their house. When they asked for her help in selecting some new summer porch furniture, she also advised them on decorating the adjacent hallway so the new furniture they selected would fit in better with their overall decorating scheme.

2. Take the Initiative in Solving Problems

Effective service-givers don't always wait for customers to bring in their problems. If they know the customer might be having a problem with their product or service, they contact the customer right away to let them know about it. They try to solve the problem as best they can, and if they are unable to, they take the initiative in helping the customer find a solution to the problem. They never say, "Sorry, that's not our problem," even when the problem isn't their fault. They act responsibly by trying to help customers get their problems solved, no matter whose fault the problem was.

Diana Green worked in her father's beauty shop. Sometimes when things were running late, she called customers who were scheduled to come in later that day and told them of the delay. She asked them if they wanted to change appointments, or she suggested they come in later than they had originally been scheduled. This made sure customers didn't experience long, unpleasant waits for service and allowed them to use their time more effectively. The customers always appreciated this kind of service.

3. Do the Job Carefully the First Time

Quality service-givers try to minimize errors and the time-consuming, costly need to do something over or correct a mistake. They are fast and efficient, but take time to check carefully to see that the work is done correctly the first time.

Carla Young had worked in the Passport Application office of the post office for nearly ten years. She knew that errors in filling out the application form could result in lengthy delays for her customers and her own department. After each customer had completed the application and brought it back to her, she checked it over carefully, line by line, to make sure that it was all okay.

4. Keep Their Promises

Honesty and integrity are important to quality service-givers. That's why they never make promises they are unable to keep. And they always keep the promises they do make. Many customers are given easy promises in order to make them feel good, get rid of them, etc. Later, when these promises are not kept, they get angry, distrustful and lose faith in the service-giver and the organization. Quality service-givers know this and work hard to maintain their reputation for honesty and integrity.

Larry Herschel ran a florist shop. He had not missed a promised delivery date in the 12 years he had been in business. Often he made deliveries himself after hours just to maintain his reputation of keeping his promises to his customers. He felt a lot of his business came from customers who had faith in his ability to deliver flowers as promised.

5. Keep Customers Informed

One of the skills quality service-givers develop quickly is that of keeping customers informed about what is happening. A good service-giver never leaves the customer wondering what's going on now? What's happening? What comes next? Good service-givers tell their customers **what** they are doing and **why**, and what they can expect will happen next. This helps make the service transaction pleasant and anxiety-free for the customer.

Rose Adams, an eighty-seven year old woman, was traveling alone and missed her flight connections. Dale Custer, an airline representative, took care of her. He carefully explained what he would do, then got busy arranging other flights for her, calling her daughter to let her know what had happened and checking on Mrs. Adams' luggage. Every few minutes he went over to where Mrs. Adams was sitting and told her what had happened so far and what he was doing. Mrs. Adams was anxious but felt comforted as a result of Dale's keeping her informed.

D. Coping With Customer Problems

1. Stay Cool in a Crisis

One of the most remarkable traits of quality service-givers is their ability to stay cool, calm and collected in a crisis. That's one of their outstanding features. They realize even when everything is in an uproar, it doesn't do much good to panic. They know they are unable to give their best efforts if they are screaming and shouting or fussing and fuming. Effective service-givers have come to learn if they hang in there in a crisis situation, and stay cool, others around them tend to settle down a bit. Then things seem to go a lot easier for everyone.

Joy England was a desk clerk with a major airline at O'Hare airport. When a huge blizzard struck Chicago one January, the airport was suddenly in chaos. At her counter, hundreds of people lined up, some crowding and shoving, waving tickets, demanding information, etc. Through it all, Joy remained calm. She worked quickly and efficiently, but concentrated on one person at a time. As people at the desk watched her quiet efficiency, even in the midst of a total crisis, they calmed down. A few passengers tried to control some of the rowdier ones to help Joy out so she could do her job.

2. Take a Positive Approach to Complaints

Complaints are opportunities for organizations to improve their services. With that understanding, good service-givers see complaints as normal, useful parts of any service-giving activity. They handle complaints quickly and effectively and are not afraid of them or try to avoid them. Of course, quality service-givers are never happy to see their customers complain because it may mean a breakdown in the service that was given. But when there are complaints, they take a positive, helpful, problem-solving approach. They handle them in such a way that customers who are satisfied with the way the complaint was handled, often become even better customers because of it.

Whenever people brought in their cars with a complaint, Jack Armstrong, the Service Manager, would say to the customer, "I'm sorry you have a complaint, but I am pleased that you have given us a chance to put it right for you." His confident, reassuring manner often made unhappy customers feel better. They were sure that the complaint would be properly taken care of. This was especially true when Jack followed up by carefully listening to the customer's complaint before taking action.

II Service-Givers and Their Organization

1. Know Their Organization

Effective service-givers know and understand their organization, what it does and how it works. They are familiar with its products and services, understand its aims and objectives, and know the organization's history and reputation. With such an understanding, they can carry out their responsibilities more effectively.

2. Understand Their Job Authority and Responsibility

In a service organization, everyone has a high degree of responsibility for giving good service. But not everyone has the same level of authority in their job. Good service-givers know how much authority they have and don't try to go beyond it.

Quality service-givers also understand something else that's very important. They know it is their job to follow established policies and procedures. But from time to time, customers will want someone higher up in the organization to deal with their problem. Quality service-givers know the answer the customer might get could be different from what they told them while following policy. But they are happy to quickly and courteously help customers contact people in the organization with higher authority.

There are often good reasons for these "exceptions" and quality service-givers understand this. They don't let these situations throw them or make them angry or resentful. They understand this is management's job to make exceptions from time to time from established policies and procedures. They know even after an exception, policies and procedures, unless changed, are still valid and they, as good service-givers, should continue to follow them in day-to-day operations.

Bill Galloway handled customers for a payroll services company. When a customer called to turn in a payroll after the deadline, Bill explained that payrolls couldn't be taken after 4:00 p.m. on Thursdays. The customer got upset and wanted to talk to Bill's manager. Bill explained the policy and the fact that he couldn't authorize an exception, but quickly gave the customer his manager's name and transferred the call immediately. Later, Bill's manager told him why an exception had been made, and Bill understood this was only an exception, and the 4:00 p.m. closing deadline on Thursday was still the policy.

3. Represent Their Organization Well

To customers, service-givers **ARE** the organization. How service-givers look, act and talk, projects an "image" of their organization. How service-givers actually perform helps create their organization's reputation.

When customers talk about the service they received, rarely do they refer to the one service-giver they might have dealt with. They usually talk as though **that** service-giver was the whole organization. Quality service-givers realize if they represent their organization well, customers will come back and use their services again. They also realize if they **don't** represent their organization well, the customer may **never** want to deal with that organization again.

4. Balance Customer and Organization Needs

Every service organization has to maintain a balance between its own needs and those of its customers. To meet **all** the needs and demands of the customers might mean an organization would soon go out of business. But **not** to respond to the needs and wants of customers may bring the same result. Quality service-givers are able to strike a balance between these two needs. They know that the organization's needs have to be met. But they know customers' needs must be met, too, if the organization is to survive.

5. Work Effectively With Their Manager

Everyone has a manager, and quality service-givers are no exception. They have learned to work well with their manager. They know they must keep their manager informed whether the information is good or bad. They know, too, they should not bring their manager a problem without some alternative solutions and their recommendation as to what should be done. And good service-givers know which problems should be brought to their manager and which ones they should handle themselves.

They also realize that understanding their job responsibilities and their level of authority is critical. If they have a question regarding these, they quickly get it cleared up with their manager.

6. Welcome Feedback on Their Performance

Effective service-givers like to know how well they are doing. They appreciate customer surveys and other kinds of feedback so they can hear about the things they do well and pinpoint the weaknesses in their performance. They also appreciate getting performance evaluations from their manager. They want to know what will help them improve the service they are offering their customers.

7. Work Well With Other Service-Givers

Quality service-givers are good team players. They cooperate with other service-givers in their own organization. They are constantly asking, "What do other people in my organization need from me to be effective?" They try to do whatever is necessary to contribute to the success of other parts of their organization. With tact and diplomacy, they are also quick to let other people in the organization know what they, as quality service-givers, need from them in order to do a better job.

At the Harvard Paper company, there were five men in the Customer Service Department. They worked as a team, even though each person was assigned their own customers. They backed each other up, were careful to take good messages for one another, and made sure they all looked out for the organization's customers by looking out for each other. They also met every so often with the Sales Department and with Shipping and Receiving to find ways they could improve overall customer service.

8. Help Identify Service System Problems

Quality service-givers are the eyes and ears of a service organization. They are in constant contact with customers and know what annoys them and what prevents the organization from giving good service. They note these barriers to good service, and make sure they tell the right people about them so they can be changed or corrected. They ask questions like, "Is there any way we can make this service faster and more efficient? Is there any way we can make this service more convenient for our customers?" Even though all their suggestions and ideas for improvements might not be accepted, quality service-givers keep up a steady search for ways things can be improved.

How To Use This Material

You can use the preceding material to evaluate your own performance as a service-giver. Chances are, as you read through this list, you discovered many things you already do well.

For those areas where you feel you might do better, the following chapters of this book will give you many specific, "how to" techniques. You'll find these very helpful in your efforts to improve your performance.

In the future you can use this list of what superior service-givers do in another way. By reviewing the material from time to time you can refresh your memory and help sustain your professional level of service-giving.

You might also find this list helpful in evaluating the service you receive from others. As you go to the bank, travel, visit your doctor's office or shop, use the list to become more aware of the quality of service you are getting. As you begin to be more conscious of the service others are giving you, you will find that you become more aware of your own performance as a service-giver. This, too, can help you reach and sustain a superior level of service-giving in your job.

What Do Quality Service-Givers Do?

My research with thousands of service-givers, in hundreds of different service organizations, indicates that superior service-givers have unique qualities and characteristics.

These fall into two groups:

I   **Service-Givers and Their Customers**

   A. **Attitudes Toward Customers**

   * Enjoy helping people
   * Handle people well
   * Care for their customers
   * Give fair and equal treatment to all
   * Never use their job authority to "punish" people

   B. **Skills in Dealing with Customers**

   * Know the technical parts of their job
   * Follow a consistent method of giving service
   * Reassure people about their service
   * Communicate effectively
   * Refer people when necessary
   * Always use courtesy
   * Are neat, clean and well-organized
   * Use the telephone effective
   * Help educate customers

   C. **Preventing Customer Dissatisfaction**

   * Anticipate customer needs
   * Take the initiative
   * Do the job carefully the first time
   * Keep their promises
   * Keep customers informed
   * Handle people well

D. Coping With Customer Problems

* Stay cool in a crisis
* Take a positive approach to complaints

II Service-Givers and Their Organization

* Know their organization
* Understand their job authority and responsibility
* Represent their organization well
* Balance customer and organization needs
* Work effectively with their manager
* Welcome feedback on their performance
* Work well with other service-givers
* Help identify service system's problems

4.
Communicating with Customers

Every service-giving job calls for the use of communications skills: listening, talking, writing or reading. Quality service depends on service-givers demonstrating effectiveness in all four areas. In your job as a service-giver, some of these communications skills may be used less frequently than others. For instance, most of your work might be on the phone, and you seldom write to customers. Or perhaps your job requires communicating with customers mostly by letter, and you rarely talk to them directly, either by phone or in person.

Whatever your particular job situation, read these over carefully. Check yourself to see how you are doing. If you are in doubt, ask others to help by giving you some feedback.

The important thing to realize is giving quality service depends heavily on the use of the following effective communication skills.

Listening

By far the most important communications skill for you to develop is listening. On the average, you will spend 9% of your time at work writing, 16% reading, 25% talking and 50% listening!

Research shows most of us don't listen very well. The average person is only able to effectively retain about 25% of what they hear. But by learning to utilize better listening techniques, we can increase that percentage to 85% or 95%!!

Part of the reason we find listening difficult is because we can hear at the rate of about 500 words per minute, but most of us speak at only about 125 words per minute! It is hard to keep our minds on what other people are saying when there is that sort of time gap.

But there's another reason, too. We grow up with the idea listening is just passive, and we can best get what we want in the world by talking, not listening. But effective listening is far from passive. As you read over these techniques for better listening, you'll see how much attention and hard work is required for good listening!

Why Listen?

There are many benefits for a service-giver in using effective listening techniques. First, you'll get the information you need from customers and other service-givers. This will help you be more effective, avoid mistakes and problems and consistently give quality service.

Second, when you listen it does a great deal for the customer. It shows them you consider them important and worthwhile, and you are interested in them and their problems.

It also helps customers develop trust and confidence in you and more easily accept what you have to say.

When you listen to others properly, they are better able to listen to themselves. And when people really hear what they are saying, they often begin to change their attitude and, in some cases, even change their demands.

Listening helps defuse emotions and anger. Few of us can manage to stay angry in the face of sincere, active listening on the part of the person to whom we are complaining.

Good listeners are rare. Your customers and fellow service-givers will be much more impressed with you if you can use some of the listening techniques listed here.

How to Listen

1. **Eliminate distractions**. Turn off a noisy office machine, turn down the radio or TV, close the door, do whatever is necessary to eliminate distractions when you are listening to others.

2. **Take time to listen**. Let the other person know you are willing to take the appropriate amount of time to hear them out, to listen fully to what they have to say.

3. **Listen fully.** Every message you hear contains both factual information and clues as to how the speaker feels about it.

Sometimes the most important part of the message is how the speaker **feels** about it. If a hotel customer calls room service after a one hour wait and says -

"Am I ever going to get my breakfast?"

They don't simply want a yes or no answer. They are really saying, "I am upset by having to wait so long, what's happening?"

A wise service-giver in this instance hears both the inquiry and the feelings of being upset, and responds to both.

4. **Don't get defensive.** Sometimes the message you receive is abusive and critical of you as a service-giver. Try to avoid getting defensive and fighting back. Let the other person talk and try to draw them out. Keep listening to them and you'll be able to get the conversation back on a useful track. This will keep you from interrupting the other person and starting an argument.

5. **Avoid judging the other person.** Whether they say something wrong, bad, or stupid, isn't relevant. What's important is finding out what the real problem is, and what you as a service-giver are going to do about it. Try to listen to the other person without prejudice regarding how they look or sound, where they are from, what race, religion or sex they are, etc. Concentrate on the message, not the person.

6. **"Hear" the body language.** The impact other people make on you is based only on 7% of the actual words you hear; 38% through their tone of voice, and 55% through the body language they use, primarily facial expressions in the eyes and mouth. Watching the other person carefully improves your listening. Tune in to their body position, gestures, etc.

7. **Take notes.** Don't let it interfere with your concentration on listening. But where it is important to let the other person know you want to really listen to the information they are giving you, take notes. This helps you, of course, keep track of the information you are getting. But it also helps tell the other person you are really listening.

8. **Listen for what is NOT said.** People often leave out vital information, especially if they are upset. Ask questions and note things that might have been left out.

9. **Ask questions.** This can help other people tell their story. They can be direct, fact-seeking questions, such as-

   "And what date was that?"

   Or they can be open, probing questions, such as -

   "And then what happened?"

   Questions can help determine how people feel about something and give them a chance to vent their emotions if such is necessary -

   "And how did you feel about that delivery being late?"

10. **Remain silent.** This shows the other person you are willing to keep listening. But don't wait too long if the other person doesn't pick up the conversation ball right away. Too much silence can be awkward and embarrassing.

11. **Summarize and verify.** From time to time, especially to bring the discussion back on track, say things like -

    "Now, Mr. Wilson, let me see if I understand what you are saying. Last Thursday you called the office..."

    or

    "There were three mistakes, two of which have been corrected, but there is still one we need to work on, is that right?"

    That kind of summarizing and confirming tells the other person you have been listening, and you have really heard what they were saying.

    It also allows you to take control of the dialogue, again, if they are going on too long with a tirade of emotional expression, and taking up time that could be better used to solve the problem.

12. **Reinforce and acknowledge the other person.**
Encourage them to keep talking. Nods of the head, little phrases like, "I see," " uh huh," " hmmm," that's interesting," etc., indicate **to the other person you want them to keep talking.**

13. **Be willing to risk being persuaded.** True listening means you are keeping an open mind, that you are really hearing and carefully considering what the other person is saying. Good listening shows you are actually willing to be influenced by the other person.

There is an old adage that is helpful for service-givers to remember, "You have two ears and one mouth and you should use them in that proportion - listen twice as much as you talk!"

Talking

Talking is the second communication skill to consider. Everyone knows how to talk, of course. But in quality service-giving, what you say to others, and how you say it, are critical. Consider the points below. These can help you improve your effectiveness in talking with others.

1. **Think first.** Talking comes so easily and naturally. If you are not careful, you may start talking too quickly and then try to figure out along the way what you are really trying to say. Give yourself a few seconds to pause. Organize what you plan to say and think about how you want to say it. This will help keep you out of trouble and make what you say easier for others to understand.

2. **Consider your listeners.** Consider their needs, their age, background, experience, etc. Then speak to them in terms and in ways that will be easiest for **them** to understand. Remember the old joke about the switchboard operator at the Army base? When she was called and asked what time it was, she always asked for the person's rank. When she

was asked why, she said, "If it's a regular GI, I say, "It's 1300 hours." If it's a Major, I say, "It's 1:00 p.m." And if it's a General, I say, "The little hand is pointing to 1 and the big hand is pointing to the 12."

Talk to people in ways that are best for **them** to understand. This means eliminating as much jargon from your speech as possible, especially with those customers who might not understand it.

3. **Pay close attention.** Don't try to do something else while you are talking to customers. Face them. Maintain eye contact with them. If necessary, move closer to them or go with them to another location that is less noisy. Do whatever is necessary so you can concentrate on what you are saying. Show the customer you are giving them your full attention.

4. **Talk first, paper later.** Service-givers often use forms, pamphlets, instructions, etc., with their customers or clients. The rule is, talk to the person first, **then** give them whatever paper might be involved. Review the information on the paper if necessary, but never give people a pamphlet or a paper of some kind, and then start talking. They will probably start reading the paper and won't hear you.

5. **Voice quality.** Your speech is made up of several different aspects. Check these as you talk to others to be sure your quality of voice is what you want it to be:

Tone - The word "Hmmm" can be used to express at least six different meanings, just by changing your tone of voice. Our emotions are expressed primarily through our voice. Anger, joy, fear ... all can be "heard" by others in just the tone of the voice you use.

Speed - Speaking either too slowly or too fast can be a serious distraction for the listener. Check out your voice speed with others, make sure it is well within the "normal" range with which other people will be comfortable.

Volume - Talking too loudly or too softly can also make it difficult for your listener. The most interesting speech pattern, and the one easiest to listen to, is a voice pattern with variety in both speed and volume.

Accent - If you have a noticeable accent in your pronunciation, be alert to the fact others might have a hard time understanding you. Slow down or spell out any words that might cause a problem. Try to use another phrase to clarify your meaning. Remember, some people might not understand you, but are too shy to ask you to explain what you said.

Pronunciation - Try to pronounce your words clearly and sharply to avoid misunderstanding. Don't be lazy. The phrase "You could have" is liable to come out "Yacooda" if you are not careful to articulate properly.

6. **Use visual aids.** Many people are more visual than oral. They can understand things better if they can see a chart, diagram, sketch, map, etc. You can help insure understanding when you are talking to someone else by using some kind of visual aid.

7. **Terminology.** Every service-giving organization has its own "language" using special terms which are not familiar to others. This "jargon" makes sense only when you are talking with other service-givers who understand the language.

But when you talk with customers, try not to use terminology that doesn't make sense to them. If you do, take time to explain the meaning of the terms you use. Avoiding the use of terminology customers don't understand is also a form of courtesy. It is usually intimidating and discomforting for a customer to hear a lot of terms and phrases that are strange to them. And remember, most of your customers probably will not speak up and ask you to explain.

8. **Avoid assumptions**. When you talk to your customers, try to avoid making assumptions about what they know or don't know or about what they need. Most people will be reluctant to interrupt you and challenge your assumption if it is wrong.

9. **Two general rules.** Here are two things that can help you be more effective in talking with other people:

    Avoid generalizations. Try not to use words like "all," "always," and "every time." Such words are rarely accurate and often cause customers to lose credibility in what you are saying and then become argumentative and defensive.

    Avoid inflammatory words and phrases. Try to avoid using words and phrases that would be challenging, insulting and intimidating for your customers. Here are a few examples of words and phrases that service-givers sometimes use, and the implications of each:

    "That's never happened before." (Implication - you as the customer must have messed up, we are perfect)

    "No one else had this problem." (Implication - something is wrong with you, all our other customers are okay)

    "You should have told us that earlier." (Implication - you as the customer are at fault, what's the matter with you?)

    Often service-givers blurt out these things without first thinking through the impact on the customer. Check your own use of these kinds of phrases. Substitute ones that are less inflammatory and that won't start an argument with your customer.

10. **Ask for feedback.** As you talk to other people, watch for their reaction. If you get some signals your customer isn't listening, seems confused or is having a hard time understanding you, stop. Check it out. Ask questions like -

    "Does that make sense to you?"

    "Am I going over this too fast? Too slow?"

    "Are some of these terms confusing to you?"

If you feel these kinds of "checking" questions might make the customer feel as though you don't think they're too bright, here's a way to handle that. Phrase the question so that you are checking on **your** ability to communicate, not on their ability to listen. Here are some examples:

"Just to make sure I haven't gone over this too fast, Mrs. Wilson, can you tell me what you understand we're going to do next?"

"I might have used some terms here I didn't explain very well, Mr. Withers, are there any of these terms I could explain better?"

This way, the client may feel a lot less intimidated and be more willing to speak up to clarify any misunderstandings.

In talking to others, remember what you are up against. Research shows the average person is not a very good listener and will probably be able to retain no more than 25% of what you say. By being careful when you talk to your customers, however, you can increase that percentage and help them better understand and accept what you are saying.

Writing

The third communication skill you need to develop is the ability to write well. Like talking, all of us can write. But to do it well requires a little more thought and practice than most of us are willing to give.

The first requirement for effective writing is legibility. If you write something by hand, other people **must** be able to decipher it! Taking time to write carefully and legibly is critical. And if you are sending someone copies, the copies also have to be legible and easy to read.

Finding the right time and place for writing is important, too. Effective writing takes time to think through, outline, edit and proofread, and you need to have a comfortable, well-lighted area where you can be free of interruptions for at least a little while. You should keep writing supplies close at hand and a spelling dictionary to use regularly.

For some reason, when people start to write they sometimes get very formal and stuffy. They start using big words and long, awkward phrases. People often write to impress others rather than to communicate. Consider these two phrases, which one would you rather try to figure out?

"Those tools are not the right ones for doing that repair work."

"It is not within the realm of feasibility that the aforementioned mechanical devices can have repairs effected upon them by these specific and precise instruments."

A good rule to follow is write as you talk. Imagine your reader is right there with you. Talk to them in a straightforward, friendly and helpful way, then write the same way. That trick alone can greatly improve your writing!

It is helpful to remember all writing carries with it more than just the message intended. "What" we say may consist of facts and data, straightforward information. But "how" we say it creates the tone of the writing and may convey attitudes and feelings the reader quickly picks up.

The trick of effective writing is to make sure the factual message you are sending is clearly understood, and the tone of your communication conveys the right attitude and feeling. Good writing consists of paying attention to both **WHAT** you say, and **HOW** you say it, so your reader doesn't hear an unintended, negative message that might make them think you don't care about them, or you don't like them, etc.

For service-givers representing their organizations, there is another aspect of writing to be carefully considered. Because writing becomes a permanent record, it is frequently used as "proof" of something that occurred or didn't occur. You need to keep in mind the importance of any writing that might become a permanent record. Such a record can be helpful to the organization in any legal dispute, showing that certain things were told to customers.

It can also be used against the organization as a liability, and for that reason, service-givers need to be careful of what they commit to in writing. In particularly sensitive areas where a possibility of legal liability is involved, service-givers should check with their manager or a legal department to make sure that what they are committing to a permanent written record is something that will not be harmful to the organization at some later date.

Here is a step-by-step approach to writing that will be helpful to you. Each of the steps is important and can help you avoid costly mistakes or misunderstandings in sending written messages to others.

Step One - Consider the Purpose of Your Writing

What is it that you are trying to accomplish? Inform? Confirm? Explain? Persuade? Request? Think about **why** the written message is being sent. Keep in mind, too, other purposes such as maintaining customer goodwill, improving the organization's image, maintaining the organization's reputation, etc.

Step Two - Consider the Reader

Who will be reading your writing? What do you know about them? Where and when will they be reading your written message? What do you guess their attitudes or feelings will be? Can you anticipate anything that would cause them to misunderstand, get angry, get confused? Will they understand the terms you are using?

By thinking through **WHO** will be reading your written message, you can empathize with your reader and send your message to them in a way they can easily understand: one that will convey a friendly, helpful and courteous attitude.

Step Three - Determine the Scope of the Message

This is to make sure your message is complete as well as clear and concise. Using seven questions can often help you make sure you have covered all the bases. These seven questions are contained in a little verse you might want to memorize:

"Seven honest-serving men
 Taught me all I ever knew;
 Their names are simply why, when
 How, how much, what, where and who."

Check out each question - is it relevant for your written message? If so, make sure your message gives the reader the answer to each question. That will help ensure your message has dealt with everything that needs covering.

Step Four - Outline Your Message

Good writing is good thinking. Take time to outline your ideas before starting to write. Make sure the most important part of your message comes first, and the details follow. Spending more time in outlining and thinking through your message can reduce the amount of time you actually have to spend writing, and makes the task of writing easier.

Step Five - Follow These Guidelines for Good Writing

a. Write as you talk, using a natural, friendly, helpful and courteous tone.

b. Use short sentences, try for an average of 14-17 words per sentence. Longer sentences can probably be broken up and rewritten as several brief sentences.

c. Use short, simple, easily understood words. Avoid jargon and terminology with which others might not be familiar. If you have to use technical terms for preciseness, follow them with explanations "lay" people can understand.

d. Use "helpers" to make it easier for the reader to read your message. Use paragraphs, lists, tables, numbering, indentations, heading and subheadings.

e. Use fewer words.
Write, "April" not "the month of April."
Write, "$39.50" instead of "in the amount of $39.50."

f. Be specific and use precise words whenever possible.

Instead of writing, "We will keep you informed" write "I will telephone you."

Many words are subject to different interpretations and have different meanings. Try to use words and phrases that are precise in their meaning.

g. Use the active voice, not passive.
Write, "We will send" not "it will be sent by us."

h. Use the same courtesy words and phrases you would use in speaking directly with the reader. You'll find a list of these in the courtesy section of this book.

Step Six - Edit Your Writing

Few of us can write and have it be really effective the first time. We need to edit and re-write what we do, to make it clear and easy to understand. All good writers develop this skill knowing their first "inspired" effort is usually not what they will end up with.

Step Seven - Proofread

As you don't want to appear in front of customers with smudgy dirt on your face, buttons missing from your clothing or messy hair, you don't want your writing to appear to them in the same way. Typos, misspelled words, smudges, and omissions all can be avoided with careful proofreading. If it is something complicated and very critical, have someone else help you proof your writing.

Reading

This is the skill least attended to. We assume we all know how to read. Yet, every day costly mistakes are made in service-giving because someone didn't read a document carefully or thoroughly. Here are some tips that can help you stay out of trouble.

1. **Prepare for reading.** Try to have a comfortable place for the reading you must do in your job. Be sure there is good lighting, you have a dictionary handy, and you have a space where you can take notes and write. Try to avoid interruptions. If you are interrupted, be sure to go back to your reading carefully, perhaps going back and starting all over.

2. **Read documents twice.** First, read the document all the way through slowly enough to understand the overall message, but not in detail. The purpose here is to understand the overall content and intent of the document. Check to be sure you are the right person to be reading it.

Also keep in mind **why** you are reading it and generally what you will be doing with it.

Then read it again in detail, slowly. Note those areas in particular where you are involved and action is required. Mark the document. Underline or use a yellow highlighter. If the document is a file document, make a copy of it, and then mark up your own copy.

3. **Read aloud whenever you can.** The act of speaking as you read gets you involved in the reading and helps avoid the possibility of skipping over things, missing them, etc. If your work situation doesn't permit reading aloud, move your lips or speak softly. Your school teachers might have told you, "Don't move your lips when you read." Forget that! Mumbling and lip moving will help you be a more effective reader!

4. **Decide what is to be done with the document.** Should it be filed, sent to others, etc. Then note somewhere what you did with it. Later, if you need to go back to it, you'll be able to trace its whereabouts. Also, you'll be able to tell others what you did with it when you handled it.

5. **Check out misunderstandings**. Never assume you know. When in doubt - check it out! Look up the word, don't be lazy. Check out the meanings of terms you don't understand. Check with the sender of the document if you are confused. Discuss it with others, get their ideas on what the document says. Often, we can read the words ... but due to the writer's approach, we don't understand the meaning. Nail it down, be sure you understand. Much of what you may be reading will come to you from others in your organization. Whenever you are in doubt about their intended meaning, check it out.

6. **Don't get hooked on angry, emotional words.** If a letter says, "Your lousy, stupid company messed me up again"...try not to let that get to you. If you, in turn, get angry or emotional, your ability to read carefully will be impaired.

41

7. **Don't waste time on judging the writer.** If you get a document with misspellings, smudgy paper, scrawly handwriting, etc., you may be tempted to judge the writer as stupid, lazy or not worth bothering about. Be careful! There may be valuable information, useful ideas or important data there. You don't want to overlook it because you think the writer is someone not worth bothering about.

8. **Be careful with critical items.** After the first two readings for general content and detail, set it aside for a day or two. Even a few hours is helpful if you are unable to give yourself several days. Then look at it again. Also, you might have someone else read it, too. You can help eliminate the risk of errors and omissions that way. For critical documents, the extra effort will be well worthwhile.

9. **Use your imagination.** What is **NOT** said may be vital. Ask yourself, "Is there something else that **SHOULD** be here and isn't?" Try to be empathetic. Go beyond the actual document. What is the customer concerned about? What are the larger issues and purposes? This may help you pinpoint things you need to ask about, check out, etc., that are **NOT** in the letter or document you are reading.

As you read through this chapter you probably came across many things you've heard before. But we all need to be reminded of these communications skills since they are so critical in dealing effectively with others. You might find it helpful in the future to read over this chapter every so often and remind yourself of these skills. By refreshing your memory from time to time and practicing them frequently, you'll develop your ability to listen, talk, write and read more effectively. This in turn can be of great value to you in improving your ability to deal with customers and others working with you.

Communicating With Customers

Quality service-giving depends on effective listening, talking, writing and reading. Face-to-face, telephone and written communications must be complete and accurate. Communication with customers and fellow service-givers can be improved by better:

Listening

About 50% of your job requires listening, but most people retain only about 25% of what they hear. Listening is not a passive activity, it requires attention, concentration and hard work. Listening offers you great benefits because it:

* Helps get full and complete information
* Avoids mistakes and problems
* Shows customers you consider them important
* Show you are interested in helping customers solve problems
* Helps customers develop trust and confidence in you
* Makes it easier for customers to accept what you have to say
* Helps customers listen to themselves and possibly change unreasonable demands
* **Helps diffuse emotions and anger**

How to Listen

* Eliminate distractions
* Take time to listen
* Listen fully
* Don't get defensive
* Avoid judging the other person
* "Hear" the body language
* Take notes
* Listen for what is **NOT** said
* Ask questions
* Use silence
* Summarize and verify
* Reinforce and acknowledge
* Be willing to risk being persuaded

Talking

What you say and **how** you say it greatly influences your success in dealing with customers. You can help customers better understand, remember and accept what you say if you:

* Think first before talking
* Consider your listener
* Pay close attention
* Talk first, handle papers later
* Control your voice quality, including -
    -tone
    -speed
    -volume
    -accent
    -pronunciation
* Use visual aids
* Avoid confusing terminology
* Avoid assumptions and generalizations
* Avoid inflammatory words and phrases
* Ask for feedback

Writing

Writing is another very important way you communicate with your customers. There is a high potential for misunderstanding in written communications because you have no chance to confirm that the other person has received and understood your message. To increase your effectiveness in written communications follow these guidelines:

* Write legibly and carefully
* Find the right time and place
* Minimize interruptions
* Find a comfortable, well-lighted area in which to write
* Keep supplies and a dictionary close at hand
* Don't be too formal and try to impress your reader
* Write as you talk
* Keep your writing simple and easy to understand
* Consider the "tone" of your writing as well as the facts
* Be careful when legal liability might be involved

How to Write More Effectively

Using a step-by-step approach will help you improve your writing. Follow these steps in sending written messages:

* Consider the purpose of your writing
* Consider your reader
* Determine what is to be covered in your message
* Outline first
* Use short sentences
* Use short, simple and easy-to-understand words
* Avoid jargon and confusing technical terminology
* Use "helpers" like paragraphs, lists, numbering, headings, sub-headings, indentations
* Use as few words as possible
* Use precise words, be specific
* Use the active voice
* Edit your writing
* Proofread your message before sending

Reading

Costly mistakes, delays and confusion can occur when you fail to read letters and documents carefully. Reading is a critical skill that can be developed. Use these ideas to help improve your reading:

* Prepare carefully for reading
* Read documents twice
* Read aloud whenever possible
* Carefully consider what is to be done with a document after reading
* Check carefully for possible misunderstandings
* Don't get hooked on angry, emotional words
* Don't judge the writer
* Handle critical, complicated items very carefully
* Use your imagination

5. The Importance of Courtesy

Using courtesy at all times is the mark of a truly professional service-giver. Far from being something "nice" or "extra" you do for customers, it is a basic, essential part of quality service-giving.

But courtesy should never become routine or mechanical. Courtesy phrases like "Thank you" or "Come back and visit us again," if delivered without feeling, are actually the signs of mediocre or poor service. True courtesy is always an expression of a real feeling toward customers, a sincere appreciation of their needs and gratitude for their business.

Real "pros" at service-giving are courteous with customers regardless of the transaction at hand. Even when you are unable to give a customer exactly what they want, or even when you are dealing with an angry, irate customer, using courteous behavior is a must.

Manners and Courtesy

Historically, courtesy was deference toward royalty and the upper classes. It was a way lower-level people could show their subservience to their king or to their masters.

Gradually, these "courtesies" began to be identified with the upper classes as manners and "good behavior." It was felt if you were a "better" member of society, you used good manners. You ate, spoke and dressed "properly" and demonstrated "refined" behavior as you went about your business and came in contact with others.

Today, courtesy still has some of its historical roots, but has come to mean a way we can show care, empathy and concern for those around us. It is a way of showing others you appreciate them, you recognize their needs and wants, and you are concerned about their welfare.

Being courteous to one another is a way we have of smoothing out all the rough spots in our daily contacts with others. It makes all our transactions go forward more easily, and makes everyone feel more comfortable with one another. Being courteous is **NOT** a sign of weakness or servility toward others. In many ways a service-giver who uses courtesy, even in situations where there is conflict and hostility, shows a superior character and a commitment to high, professional standards.

As our modern society has become more complicated, as the pace has picked up, some people neglect to pay attention to courtesy. They feel because things are moving so fast and are so chaotic, it is permissible to be rude or to forget good manners. Quality service-givers realize if courtesy phrases and behaviors become a habit with them, they can handle customers at a fast pace and still demonstrate the very best in courtesy. Professional service-givers don't "forget" courtesy regardless of the circumstances.

Benefits of Being Courteous

As I mentioned earlier, many service-giving organizations are characterized by their similarities. Banks, hospitals, car rental agencies, travel agencies, airlines - all of them often offer customers the same type of services and at about the same costs. Sometimes the only distinguishing difference between two service organizations is the courteous behavior of their representatives. In one bank you can go in and be met with courteous, friendly behavior. In another bank you are met with no sign of recognition, no friendly greetings and no expression of appreciation for your business. And in yet another bank, you may be met with rude behavior, an unnecessary wait and expressions of hostility if you ask for anything extra.

When you are courteous to customers, the benefit to your organization will be enormous. It may be the major reason your organization is superior to similar, competing organizations.

There are also many benefits to customers when you are courteous. Their transaction is made more pleasant. They feel better about you, your organization and themselves. They also enjoy telling others of the pleasant experiences they have had with you and your **organization**.

Another benefit in using courtesy is to yourself. First, you can take great pride and satisfaction from the fact you are handling your job as a service-giver like a real "pro." You are living up to the standards of quality service which call for using courtesy at all times with customers, fellow service-givers and other members of your own organization.

There is also another benefit: courteous behavior is contagious. When you are friendly and polite, truly sincere in trying to understand and care about your customers, your customers will likely behave toward you the same way. Even when customers come in with a chip on their shoulder, angry and ready to fight, when they encounter true courtesy they calm down and begin to respond in kind. They get more reasonable and easier to deal with. That makes your job easier every time.

Another reason why being courteous pays off for you is that it has become a rare commodity in today's world. People are not always rude and rough with each other, but they often forget to make things a little more pleasant by being courteous. When your customers come across your courteous words and behaviors, it's rare and they appreciate it. They will more than likely tell you about it. When you are courteous, your chances of hearing "Thank you, I really appreciate your help" are greatly increased. And that will feel good to you. They'll tell others, too, including people higher up in your organization. Most customers like to feel good about their choice of organizations. When they are treated courteously, they enjoy telling you how much they appreciate it and telling others about you.

A further benefit to you as a service-giver in using courtesy is it builds goodwill that may come in handy later on. If your customers have had pleasant encounters with you over a long period of time, when they do have a complaint or a problem, they come to you in a much more reasonable way, sometimes apologizing to you for bringing up a problem!

Courtesy also tends to open up communication channels. It helps people be more open, more forthright, more honest. Being courteous and polite and caring with your customers, means that they will be more willing to share information with you. Information that could help you do a better job. It may be negative or positive feedback, but the important thing is they are willing to talk to you.

For instance, suppose you made a mistake in a transaction with one of your customers. And it was a costly one in their favor. A customer who has been treated kindly and with sincere courtesy will tend to bring it to your attention and avoid a problem for you later on. A customer who feels they have been treated indifferently or rudely in the past may keep silent, leaving you with a problem later on when you discover the mistake.

What is Real Courtesy?

Courtesy consists of three things: attitude, phrases and behavior. All of them have to be present for true courtesy to take place. For instance, if you say the right words, but rudely turn your back, that's not courtesy. If your attitude really is, "These customers are a real pain in the neck," but you try to use courtesy words with them, it will come across as phony.

Real courtesy consists of an attitude of concern and caring for your customers, and an understanding of their needs and wants. It is an attitude that says, "You are important to me as a customer and I appreciate your business." It is an attitude of taking pleasure in helping others, even when they are not as courteous and polite as they might be.

But courtesy is also the use of accepted words and phrases. The list below shows just a few of them. Look it over. Develop phrases and words you feel would be appropriate for your service-giving situation and use them regularly.

Courtesy Words and Phrases

Please
Thank you
Use the customer's name frequently, check to be sure you are pronouncing it correctly
I'm very sorry
Excuse me
Friendly greetings: Hello, Good Morning, Goodbye
You're welcome
We appreciate your business
I'd be happy to do that for you

May I help you please?
I'm sorry to keep you waiting
Thank you for waiting
It was nice talking to you
Is there anything else I can do for you?
Thanks for calling
It's been a pleasure helping you

Courtesy also consists of behaviors. Often what you **do** as a service-giver says more than the words or phrases you speak. "Actions speak louder than words" was never truer than in customer relations. Looking at people, smiling, making eye contact, pausing in your work to pay attention to them, standing up when you meet customers...all these are powerful communications and mean as much or more than whatever you might say.

Again, check the partial list below. Think of your own service-giving situation and your behavior involved in greeting and dealing with your customers. Decide to really put into practice those behaviors that will demonstrate true courtesy to your customers and to your fellow service-givers.

Courtesy Behaviors

Show you are ready to help, and customers are not "interrupting" you
Keep your work area neat, clean and ready for action
Always introduce yourself
Show that you remember people - "It's nice to have you back, "Glad to see you again," etc.
Make eye contact and smile
Don't interrupt, listen more
Invite customers to sit down
Offer refreshment
Stand up (if appropriate)
Let customers "go first"
Use "Please" whenever making a request of another person
Acknowledge people immediately, look at them and greet them
Volunteer to help: give information, ideas, suggestions or directions
Never shout or talk too loudly, or speak to customers from too far a distance

Give sincere compliments and positive feedback

Use friendly statements like, "Enjoy your meal," "Have a nice stay," "I'm sure they'll enjoy your gift," "I hope you enjoy your vacation," etc.

Act quickly

Give people helpful warnings, "Please be careful of the extension cord," "Watch that step," "Mind your head," etc.

Escort customers instead of pointing or directing them to their destination

Don't make people wait unnecessarily and apologize if you have to

Don't hurry customers

Volunteer to help co-workers

Do a little extra for the customer - offer additional services, or ask if there is anything more you could do for them

Admit and apologize for mistakes you or your organization have made

Stop what you are doing when customers approach and pay attention to them

Ask customers for their preference

Inquire about the service customers have received

Inquire about people's family, work, health, etc., if appropriate

Offer to carry, hold or store things for the customer

Keep customers informed, explain what has and will happen

When you are courteous to your customers, it is not a sign of weakness or being subservient to them. It is a mark of a truly professional quality service-giver. And, of course, the best thing you can do for your customers is to give them fast and efficient service with a courteous attitude using the appropriate words and behaviors.

The Importance of Courtesy

In the past courtesy meant deference to royalty and members of the aristocracy. In today's world it is a way of showing we are empathetic toward others, that we care about them and are looking out for their welfare. Courtesy is an essential part of giving quality service.

A truly superior service-giver remains courteous even when dealing with angry, irate customers. Remaining courteous even under the most trying circumstances is the mark of a really professional service-giver.

Routine, mechanical use of courtesy words and phrases is a mark of mediocre service. Quality service requires a sincere expression of courtesy at all times, even when the situation is chaotic and fast paced.

Benefits of Using Courtesy

* Courtesy often distinguishes your organization from others that are similar in kind
* Courtesy gives organizations a competitive edge
* Customers enjoy their experience with you and your organization and want to do business with you again
* Customers are more likely to tell others about the value of doing business with you and your organization
* You can take pride in the fact that you are doing your job in a professional manner
* It is contagious; because they are treated courteously, customers are more likely to be courteous to you
* Courtesy helps calm irate customers and make them easier to deal with
* Customers will express their appreciation and gratitude to you more often
* Courtesy builds goodwill for the future

* Courtesy encourages customers to make their complaints in a more reasonable, calm way
* Courtesy helps open up communication channels
* Courtesy encourages customers to be more open and honest
* Courtesy encourages customers to share information with you, both good and bad

What is Real Courtesy?

* A sincere attitude of concern and caring
* An understanding of customers' needs and wants
* Being polite to others even when they are not polite and courteous to you
* Using courtesy words and phrases at all times
* Understanding that courtesy "actions" often speak louder than words

6. Quality Service - The Seven-Step Method

Every service transaction is a little different. That's one of the exciting challenges of service-giving jobs, you never know what to expect. But it can also be one of the problem areas. If you are caught off guard by a customer's unusual request, or a problem they are really upset about, you may forget to use some of the quality service techniques you have learned. Or, you may get very busy and just forget some of the essential parts of a good service transaction and regret it later.

To help you with this problem, I have developed a seven-step method for giving quality service. You'll find there are several advantages to following the method in each of your service transactions:

- It will give you the confidence to effectively handle any service transaction, regardless of the situation. This is especially true if you are new to your job.
- Using a set method will help establish day-to-day consistency in your performance and that of the other service-givers in your organization.
- Using the seven-step method will also help you avoid having customer problems come up later that should have been handled in the first place.
- A regular method will also help make sure you do things correctly the first time and avoid embarrassing, costly and time-consuming errors and rework.
- By following all seven steps, you can help make sure you haven't left anything out, that you have properly covered all parts of the transaction.
- You may sometimes be surprised by customers who come at you in unexpected ways. Using the seven-step method will help you cope effectively with this kind of surprise and keep you in control of the situation despite possible disruptions and distractions from the customer.
- The seven-step method is also flexible and you can use it with customers either in face-to-face transactions or on the telephone.

I designed the seven-step method to apply to most service transactions. However, your job situation might be unique and you may want to adapt it so it will better fit your particular organization.

If you feel you want to adapt the method, discuss it with your manager and other service-givers with whom you work. Once you've worked out a step-by-step method you feel will work for you, write it up and follow it in all of your service transactions. It will help you give your customer quality service each and every time, regardless of circumstances.

Step One - Create a Friendly, Courteous Climate

You can do this in several ways. First of all, smile and look at the customer. Try to use the customer's name as much as possible. Introduce yourself. Greet your customer in a cheerful and friendly manner. Take time to reassure them they will be given prompt, efficient service.

Using courtesy words and phrases throughout the service transaction is a must. (Review the courtesy section of this book.) Avoid indicating any signs of boredom, impatience or dissatisfaction with the customer's actions or reactions. Remember, courtesy is contagious and causes customers to act courteously in return.

In on-going relationships with customers where you have had repeated contacts with them, acknowledge this and recognize their continued patronage. Where appropriate, invite them to sit down, be sure they are comfortable and feel welcome.

Step Two - Get Necessary Information by Listening and Asking Questions

Routine service transactions can sometimes lead you to assume you have all the information needed to proceed. Making these assumptions is hazardous. Approach each service situation carefully. Make sure you get all the information necessary to conduct an effective transaction.

This usually means listening carefully to the customer. When necessary, ask questions about any information the customer is giving you. This is particularly important when using the telephone because the possibility of miscommunication is so much higher.

Step Three - Repeat for Complete Understanding

Verifying the information with the customer is critical. Take time for this important step. It is probably the single greatest help in avoiding problems later on. You need to repeat and confirm the information the customer has given you. By doing this you continue to reassure your customer they will get the service they want.

Step Four - Propose a CAN DO Plan of Action

This step requires giving the customer several pieces of vital information. One is letting them know what your role and authority is in the transaction. If this is already known, of course you don't have to mention it. Customers really want to know **what** you **CAN DO** for them. Sometimes, they want to know **how** you are going to go about it. They want to be reassured you have the authority to act on your own, or whether they are going to have to go to someone else for approval, additional information, etc.

Propose your plan of action in terms your customer can understand. Present it in a way that offers them a satisfactory response to their need or want. Take time to make sure they fully understand what you are proposing.

Sometimes the plan of action you propose will involve **alternatives,** different things you **can do** for them. Each of these must be spelled out carefully so your customer fully understands all the **options** open to them.

It also helps to explain to customers **WHY** certain approaches are being suggested. That way they can better understand the alternatives you have offered.

Step Five - Get Agreement on WHAT is to be Done, by WHOM, WHERE, WHEN and HOW

If you give a careful explanation, your customer should have no trouble agreeing to your proposed plan of action. However, this task of getting understanding is often underestimated, and it is often only later an irate, disappointed and frustrated customer lets you know you didn't have agreement and understanding after all.

Here is where you must bring to bear all your skills of communicating effectively. Make sure you verify and confirm an understanding with your customer. If there is any doubt, you may need to carefully explain the consequences of the customer's choice, spelling out in detail what will happen as the result of the customer's choice of action.

In this step, pay attention to detail and try hard to be as **specific** as possible. "We'll have it for you next week," is not nearly as effective as, "We will deliver it to your home by 12 noon, next Wednesday, January 23rd." Doing this gives customers more confidence and reassurance you will do what you said you would do.

Step Six - Provide the Service Agreed Upon

As a quality service-giver, you must be totally committed to keeping the promises you make. Everyone has had the disappointing and frustrating experience of having service-givers make promises that were never kept. You must have a **dedicated commitment to keeping your promises** and doing what you told your customers you would do if you are going to give quality service.

Whenever a situation develops where you see the customer is not going to receive the service at a time agreed upon and as expected, you must inform them immediately. Most customers can tolerate things going wrong and understand the need for changes and adjustments in the time schedule, etc. What they are unable to tolerate is being left in the dark and not informed of the changes. A failure by service-givers to meet agreed upon deadlines, or to deliver the agreed upon service, is the primary reason customers lose confidence in service-giving organizations.

Step Seven - Follow Up to Ensure Results

In some service transactions, you may want to follow up to see that the promised service was, in fact, delivered. This is very important when you are depending on others to complete the transaction. Customer deliveries, for instance, might be made by others. You

57

need to follow up with customers to be sure the deliveries you promised them were made, and at the time agreed upon.

For many routine service transactions, follow up may not be necessary. In those cases, periodic checkups to survey your customers will be useful. Such checkups help ensure the overall service relationship continues to be a satisfactory one for the customer.

Here is an example of the seven-step method for giving quality service. The situation involves a businessman arranging a hotel meeting room for his company. He is being served by a member of the hotel's sales department. I have listed each step followed by a dialogue between the customer (Cust) and the service-giver (SG) to illustrate that step in action in a real life situation. It is somewhat abbreviated, but it will help you understand the seven-step method.

Step - One-Create a Friendly, Courteous Climate

SG: "Good morning, Mr. Baker, please come in. I'm Ella Gantry. Please sit down. Would you like some coffee?"

Cust: "Yes, thanks. I wanted to see about arranging a meeting room here at the hotel for a training session we are going to have in June."

SG: "Of course. I'm delighted you decided on our hotel and I know we can work out some arrangements with which you'll be fully satisfied."

Cust: "Well, I hope so."

SG: "Have you held any of your meetings here at the hotel before?"

Cust: "Oh, some time ago, but not recently."

SG: "Well, you'll be pleased to know we have improved our services and facilities for meetings, and I know you'll be pleased with the end result. What sort of arrangements do you require?"

58

Step Two - Get Necessary Information by Listening and Asking Questions

Cust: "Well, it's going to be a training session, we need a room for just one day. I think there will be about 25 people, we are not quite sure yet. The one thing I would like to stress is that we need a room that's the right size so we have plenty of space."

SG: "I'm sure we can arrange that, Mr. Baker. First, may I ask you a few questions to make sure I understand exactly what you need and want? Then I can help you make a choice of rooms. Later, we can take a look at the room before you make a final decision."

Cust: "Ok, what do you need to know?"

SG: "Did you have a specific date in mind?"

Cust: "Yes, June 12th, Saturday."

SG: "Now, the purpose of the meeting is a training session. Did you have a particular set-up style you wanted?"

Cust: "What do you usually do?"

SG: "Well, we can have it set up schoolroom style, all the chairs at rows of tables and facing the front. Or, we can have it set up in five round tables with five people at each table. That way you would have some of the chairs facing away from the front of the room, but the chairs are easily turned around for times when there is a presentation from the front of the room."

Cust: "There are going to be quite a few presentations, let's make it schoolroom style."

SG: "Fine. What we might also consider is having the group use break-out rooms for their discussions during the day. Would that be something you might be interested in?"

Cust: "Good idea. There will be a couple of times we want to break into small groups and that will get them out of the main room for a while."

SG: "All right, we'll set up four break-out rooms. How does that sound, Mr. Baker?"

Cust: "Fine. Oh, and we'll need a VCR and monitor, too."

SG: "Ok, we'll schedule a VCR and monitor. Will you need that for the morning or the afternoon session?"

Cust: "For the morning, but we'll need an international deck and international monitor, ½" VHS format. This will enable us to play the NTSC, PAL and SECAM broadcast standard tapes that our international delegates will be bringing with them."

SG: "I will be happy to contact our audio-visual supplier and make the request for an international deck and monitor, ½" VHS, and call you tomorrow to confirm it."

Cust: "Fine, I'll appreciate that."

SG: "Now, how about meals and coffee service?"

Cust: "Why don't we just have coffee available in the room all day long? That way our people can go get coffee whenever they want to."

SG: "Certainly. And about lunch?"

Cust: "Can we set up a group lunch near the meeting room? I want to try to keep the group together as much as possible."

SG: "Yes, of course we can. Did you want to select a specific menu?"

Cust: "No, let's have just a light buffet. I don't want them to have a big meal in the middle of the day."

SG: "That seems to be popular with a lot of groups. When I confirm all the other details with you, I'll give you a listing of what we usually serve in that sort of buffet, all right?"

Cust: "That's fine, I'll leave it up to you."

SG: "Good. Now what about timing? When do you plan to start and end the session, and what time do you want to set aside for lunch?"

Cust: "Oh, we'll probably get underway at 9 a.m. Let's have lunch at 12:30 p.m., and then we'll be out of there at around 4:30 p.m., no later than 5 p.m."

SG: "All right, Mr. Baker, you mentioned international delegates. Will you be needing any hotel rooms for them and any other participants?"

Cust: "Oh, yes, we sure will. Thank you for asking. Please make a reservation for 14 people."

SG: "Do you want them to each have a single, or will they be doubling up?"

Cust: "Oh, a single room for each one. I'll give you the names later on, okay?"

SG: "That will be fine, meanwhile I'll make room reservations for 14 the night of Friday, June 11th."

Cust: "Yes, good."

SG: "Now are there any other details we need to cover? Are there any special requirements you'll need for the room?"

Cust: "I don't think so."

SG: "Well, if there are, just give me a call. Now, let me summarize what we've talked about just to make sure I have all the details correct."

Step Three - Repeat for Complete Understanding

SG: "Your meeting will be on Saturday, June 12 for approximately 25 people. You want the room set up in schoolroom style with four break-out rooms nearby for smaller discussion groups. You need a VCR - international deck and international monitor, ½" VHS format. You want to have coffee available all day in the meeting room. Lunch will be a light buffet, served at 12:30 p.m. Your meeting will start at 9 a.m., and you expect to finish around 4:30 to 5 p.m. And I will make 14 single room reservations for your group for the night of June 11th. Is that correct?"

Cust: "That's fine. One more thing, can we set up a master account and have everything, including the room reservations, billed to my company?"

SG: "Yes, certainly. I'll make that arrangement. To whom should the invoice be sent?"

61

Cust:	"Just have it sent to my attention. Here is my card with the address, telephone and fax numbers."
SG:	"Thank you, Mr. Baker."

Step Four - Propose a CAN DO Plan of Action

SG: "Now from what you've told me, I have two suggestions. One is our Skylon meeting room on the top floor of the hotel. It is the right size and the Skylight dining room is close by for the luncheon set-up. We **can** also set up some hotel rooms on that floor for use as break-out rooms. I think you'd have privacy there and it is likely to be quiet. The disadvantage, of course, is that it is a bit out of the way. There are washrooms up there next to the meeting room, but only one telephone in the Skylight dining room.

The other choice is a regular meeting room in our conference wing. We have four small meeting rooms near it we **can** use as break-out rooms. The meeting room would be the same size as the Skylon meeting room. You would find it more convenient to the lobby, but the disadvantage is we might have a larger activity in that wing on June 12th. You would, perhaps, find it a bit more crowded and noisy."

Cust: "I think the room upstairs sounds good. We do want some privacy and quiet. I think that would be better."

SG: "I tend to agree with you. For the kind of meeting you have planned, I'm sure we **can** make you very comfortable in the Skylon Room. We'll have it set up the way we discussed, and I'll also try to make the room reservations for the people staying over on that floor of the hotel."

Cust: "Good. Anything else?"

Step Five - Get Agreement on WHAT is to be Done, by WHOM, WHERE, WHEN and HOW

SG: "I think that's it. Tomorrow I'll prepare and if you wish, fax you a confirming letter with all the details we've discussed. It will also include the name of the conference coordinator we will assign to your meeting and how you can reach her, in case you have any last minute questions. She will be at the meeting room about an hour prior to the start of your meeting, will that be okay?"

Cust: "Yes, that's fine. Well, I think we're going to have a good session. I appreciate your help...you really seem to have everything under control, and I feel confident we'll be well taken care of."

SG: "Thanks, Mr. Baker, I know you will. It's been good meeting with you. Now, before you leave, let's take a look at the Skylon Room."

Cust: "Yes, that's a good idea."

Step Six - Provide the Service Agreed Upon

In this situation, Ella Gantry did fax the confirming letter the next day. She followed that up with a phone call to Mr. Baker to make sure the letter was correct and to check to see if he had any further questions regarding the meeting. She confirmed the fact they were able to locate and would provide an international VCR deck and monitor, ½" VHS format. She wrote up all the details of the order and contacted the other appropriate members of the hotel staff. Room reservations were made and meeting preparations were completed.

Step Seven - Follow Up to Ensure Results

When the meeting came up on her follow-up calendar, she checked on preparations, and on the day of the meeting stopped in to visit Mr. Baker during the luncheon to see how things were going.

Following the meeting, Ella called Mr. Baker again to get his feedback on how the group had been handled. He had a few minor complaints which she noted. She then had a chance to encourage him to use the hotel again for any future meetings he might be planning. He indicated he would and mentioned a large sales meeting they were planning for the late fall.

As you can see from this simple situation, the seven steps are fairly easy to use. The trick is to remember they apply to **every** service transaction, not just once in a while. That way you guarantee your customers consistent, efficient quality service when they deal with you.

Quality Service -The Seven-Step Method

Every service transaction is a little different. Using the seven-step
method for giving quality service will help you maintain a
consistently superior performance regardless of the situation.

Advantages of the Seven-Step Method

* It gives you the confidence to handle any service situation
* It helps establish consistency in your performance and that of your fellow service-givers
* It helps avoid problems coming up later
* It helps you do things correctly the first time and avoid costly, embarrassing, time-consuming mistakes and rework
* It helps make sure you haven't forgotten anything
* It helps you deal efficiently with surprises and keep control of a situation despite disruptions and distractions
* It ensures quality service-giving on the telephone as well as in face-to-face customer contacts

The Seven-Step Method

1. Create a friendly, courteous climate
2. Get necessary information by listening and asking questions
3. Repeat for complete understanding
4. Propose a **CAN DO** plan of action
5. Get agreement on **WHAT** is to be done, by **WHOM, WHERE, WHEN** and **HOW**
6. Provide the service agreed upon
7. Follow-up to ensure results

7. Why Customers Get Angry

Everyone has ideas as to what **should** happen in a service transaction. These expectations are based on the customer needs discussed previously. When things don't go the way customers **think they should,** they get angry.

For instance, a customer walks into a store and sees two or three sales clerks standing nearby talking. As the customer stands there waiting, they feel as though at least one of the clerks **should** come and wait on them. The longer the customer has to wait, and the longer their expectations are not met, the more angry they become.

Or, let's say a customer goes into a restaurant and orders a meal. They feel it **ought** to arrive in a reasonable time. The longer they delay beyond the expected time, the more angry they become.

Or, perhaps a customer has been going to the same bank for five years. The customer wants to cash a check and the teller takes time to telephone to check the status of their account. The customer feels the teller **should** recognize them and not make them wait. They get angry.

All customers have the potential for getting angry. And anger involves a surge of emotion. How customers handle that anger depends on how strong the emotional surge is, and how they have learned to handle anger in the past.

How Customers Handle Anger

Basically, there are three ways customers respond to anger. I call them Position I, II and III.

Position I - Passive

In this passive position, customers usually move away from the situation. If kept waiting too long for service in a restaurant they simply walk out. If sales people don't wait on them promptly, they leave. If they are waiting in line and someone crowds in front of them, they may be angry inside, but do nothing. Later, they may take out their anger or frustration on something else, slamming a door, kicking the dog, shouting at a child, etc.

Some customers who respond to anger by taking Position I may exercise a mild form of protest. They may say things like, "I'm very disappointed," when they really mean, "I am very angry." Or they may try to use humor or sarcasm. If not waited on promptly in a store, they may say to the sales clerks, "I hope I'm not interrupting anything," in a sarcastic tone of voice. Or if someone rings for a nurse in a hospital, and the nurse finally arrives after a long delay, the patient may say, "I thought everyone had gone off duty," trying to be funny, but really just expressing their anger in a mild, more socially acceptable form.

Angry customers who choose to move to Position I can really hurt a service organization. Because they don't bother to express their feeling of anger, they just leave and take their business elsewhere. They don't give you a chance to explain or help resolve their anger and try to put the situation right. You lose customers, and you don't even know why.

Many customers choose this response because they have been taught expressing anger is wrong. They were told as children not to get upset, talk loudly or become aggressive. So when they get angry as adults, they tend to just walk away from a difficult situation to avoid any problems. Whenever possible, try to avoid having your customers get angry and just walk away.

Position II - Problem Solving

Customers who move to Position II feel it's okay to express their anger, but they do it in a positive way. They are able to say, "I am very angry about the way I have been treated, and I want someone to resolve this situation." They are emotional, but they are in control of their emotions. They are assertive and interested in finding solutions to their problem, and they want you to respond promptly to their requests.

You and your organization should be grateful for customers who get angry and choose to handle it by moving to Position II. With customers like this, you can work on the problem and find a satisfactory solution. But Position II customers need a prompt, efficient, problem-solving response. If they are not handled carefully, they may move to Position III.

Position III - Aggressive

In this position, customers get angry and lose control. Their emotions get the best of them, and they become abusive and aggressive. They may even lose sight of their goal, to get their complaint resolved, and become interested only in "getting even." Once they finish attacking something or someone they may calm down and allow their anger to subside. As their emotions quiet down, they may experience a sense of guilt and embarrassment about getting so angry and losing control.

Tim Thompson arrived late at a hotel and was told there was no record of his reservation. He blew his top, ranted and raved and began to shout to other people in the lobby that this hotel was badly managed, etc. The next day he felt embarrassed about what he had done, and sought out the night manager who had tried to help him, and apologized.

Customers who move to Position III are often people who learned early in life you could get your way if you threw a tantrum and expressed your anger in hostile, aggressive ways. Sometimes customers who normally move to Position II to handle their anger, find themselves so frustrated they lose control and move to Position III.

You, as a quality service-giver, need to remember anger is a potential response whenever people's needs are not being met. Whatever you can do to remove the possibility of frustration for your customers will help avoid potentially harmful situations where customers get angry.

Avoiding "Fight" Words

To help you stay out of trouble, here's a list of words, phrases and behaviors to avoid. Experience shows in service transactions, the use of these words and phrases often can cause customers to become angry and defensive. Not using them will help you avoid having to deal with angry customers.

1. "You" Statements

As a rule, service-givers should avoid using statements beginning with the word "you." Such statements are often perceived by the customer as judgmental, authoritarian, condescending or directive. Examples:

> **"You** must be mistaken."
> "**You** should have told me first."
> "**You can't** return that here."
> "**You'll** have to..."

2. "I" Statements

When they include a negative, "I" statements are also perceived by customers as rigid, restricting, controlling and defensive. Examples:

> "I **can't** help you."
> "I **don't** know."
> "I **won't** be here then."

3. Silence

Although this does not involve using "fight words," silence or non-responsiveness on your part can produce the same effect. Customers expect a prompt response to their complaint. When they fail to get it, they may become very angry.

4. Denials, Accusations and Refusals

> "That's never happened before."
> "No one has ever had that problem before."
> "It's the computer's fault."
> "That's not my department."
> "That's our policy, and there is nothing I can do about it."
> "Are you sure about this?"

5. "Fight" Behaviors

Sometimes it's not the words you use, but what you do. Here are some behaviors to avoid:

> Moving too slowly
> Chatting with fellow service-givers while customer waits
> Explaining what you **"CAN'T DO"**

Using a gesture rather than words to direct a customer
Turning your back on a customer without explanation
Walking away from the customer without explanation
Acting bored
Muttering obviously negative things the customer can barely hear
Sarcastic laughter
Interrupting the customer
Keeping customers on hold too long on the telephone

Try to identify some of the "fight" words, phrases and behaviors you might be using. Then substitute "problem-solving" approaches for dealing with your customers. That way you can avoid making them angry.

Why Customers Get Angry

Customers have ideas as to what should happen in a service transaction. Their needs determine their expectations. When customers' expectations are not met, they get angry. They feel they should be treated differently from how they are being handled. All customers have a potential for getting angry, which is a surge of emotion. Customers handle their anger in three different ways:

Position I - Passive

- Say nothing
- Move away from the situation
- Avoid confrontation
- Protest mildly
- Take out their anger on someone or something else
- Use sarcasm or humor

Customers who take Position I when angry often hurt a service organization because they give the organization no chance to resolve the problem. Business is lost. Customers take this position because they were taught that expressing anger was wrong or they have discovered that avoiding conflict is the path of least resistance.

Position II - Problem Solving

Customers who take this position feel that expressing anger in a positive way is good! They are helpful to organizations because they give you a chance to resolve the situation and keep their business. If not handled properly, however, these customers can easily move to Position III. Position II customers:

- Express anger positively
- Keep their emotions under control
- Assertively seek solutions to their problems

Position III - Aggressive

Customers who take this position often lose control of their emotions and may lose sight of their goal. They may become more interested in "getting even" than having their complaint resolved. After attacking you they may calm down, get their emotions under control and feel embarrassed about their behavior. Some customers take this position because they learned early in life that you can get what you want by throwing a tantrum and expressing feelings in hostile ways. Position III customers:

* Lose control of their emotions
* Demonstrate hostile, aggressive behavior
* May express their anger physically
* May be abusive to the service-giver

Avoid Making Customers Angry

* Don't use "you" statements that are judgmental, authoritarian, condescending or directive
* Don't use "I" statements that are controlling, defensive or restrictive
* Be responsive to customers, avoid inappropriate silence
* Avoid denials
* Don't make accusations
* Don't refuse to help or refer customers to others that might be able to help them
* Avoid demonstrating "fight" behaviors
* Don't explain what you **"CAN'T DO"**

8. Handling Complaints and Angry Customers

Every service organization knows the value of complaints. They provide valuable information on where things are going wrong and allow you to retain customers who might take their business elsewhere. Research shows that approximately 90% of customers who have a problem and **don't** complain, stop doing business with that organization. Approximately 50% of those customers who do complain, continue to do business with the same organization. This percentage is even higher, of course, when complaints are well handled.

Do you appreciate the value of complaints? You should. But complaints are sometimes seen by service-givers as embarrassing evidence of poor work. You might feel they are nothing but painful, awkward situations which you hope never happen. With this kind of attitude, you might approach handling complaints with fear, embarrassment and defensiveness. This probably will make you fairly ineffective in properly handling customers who do complain. It's liable to lead to such non-productive behaviors as getting defensive, being angry with and rude to customers, avoiding complaint situations, fighting with customers and even denying any involvement in the problem, desperately trying to put the blame somewhere else.

Customers, too, sometimes have negative attitudes toward complaining. They may be embarrassed at having to engage in a confrontation with you or your organization. Or they may be angry at having to take extra time and effort to solve a problem. They may be upset about the expense and inconvenience they have been put to as a result of your organization's poor performance.

Too many customers decide it is easier to handle a difficult situation simply by taking their business elsewhere. Others, due to embarrassment and anxiety, may only be able to bring themselves to complain by working themselves up into a high level of anger. They rationalize this by saying to themselves, "I have been wronged. I have a right to be angry!"

Or customers may feel powerless and fear nothing will be done about their problem unless they kick up a big fuss and rant and rave. This is especially true if their complaints have not been properly handled in the past. The result is customers often approach you with an unreasonable, highly emotional attitude which makes them much more difficult to deal with.

So, here's what you need to do. Develop two basic attitudes toward complaints. One is to see complaints as useful. Not necessarily pleasant or fun to deal with, but useful. And two, you must be understanding when you encounter anger and hostility on the part of customers. Don't allow yourself to get "hooked" by an angry customer into hostile and non-productive behavior of your own.

10-Step Method for Handling Complaints

My step-by-step method for handling complaints gives you several advantages: (1) it gives you confidence so you can cope with complaints and angry customers, (2) it promotes consistency in handling complaints and, (3) it helps make sure you can handle complaints effectively without losing customers.

Step One - Listen Without Interrupting

Regardless of how hostile, abusive and upset the customer might be, you must listen fully to the complaint without interrupting. All vital information should be written down. Listening without interrupting will also help defuse the customer's emotions. Toward the end of the customer's statements, questions to help clarify information, if necessary, are okay. But don't argue or deny anything the customer is saying, just listen.

Step Two - Don't Get Defensive

Customers may not have all the proper information. They may get abusive. They may exaggerate. They may use a loud, threatening voice. Regardless of this, you must avoid getting defensive and starting an argument. It helps to remember, although, you may not be able to do very much about your customer's improper behavior, you can understand their being upset and control your own behavior by not fighting back.

If the customer's tirade goes on too long, you can ask, "May I summarize what I understand to be the problem, and then we can try to solve it, okay?" The customer may want to continue the tirade. But if they haven't been answered with defensive, "fight" words or phrases, the chances are pretty good they are ready to settle down and listen.

Step Three - Respond with GLAD • SURE • SORRY

Next, you can use statements like: "I'm **glad** you're bringing it to our attention so I can help you. I'm **sure** we can work this out to your satisfaction. I'm **sorry** there is a problem." You need to be careful you don't immediately accept liability for the problem and say something like, "I'm sorry we have made a mistake." Until all the facts have been gathered, you are better off just to express empathy for the customer and the existence of the problem. Later, if the problem is your mistake, you can make an apology to the customer.

Step Four - Express Empathy

Next, show you understand the customer's feelings and say something like, "That (referring to the problem) must have been frustrating for you. I can understand how you might get angry and upset in that kind of situation."

This helps to further calm the customer. Once customers realize someone is able to appreciate their problem and their feelings in the matter, they are much more willing to participate calmly at working on a solution to the problem.

Step Five - Ask Questions to Understand the Problem

Once the customer has calmed down, you may discover the information they now give you may be slightly different from what they gave before. This is because the emotions involved at first may have caused them to distort or exaggerate the facts. So, you need to summarize what information you have obtained so far. Then, ask questions to get more information. Then, confirm this information with your customer. Get agreement with them on exactly what the problem is. Once this step is complete, and only then, should you go on to the next step.

74

Step Six - Find Out What the Customer Wants

What the customer wants may be obvious. If so, repeat it and ask the customer to confirm your understanding. Go the extra mile and ask, "Is there anything else you would like us to do?"

If the customer's request is not specific, ask the customer what they want you to do, or what they want to have happen regarding their complaint. In some cases, the customer may be satisfied with just "letting the organization know" what happened. Having someone listen and empathize may be all they wanted. If this is so, simply express your appreciation to your customer for telling you of their complaint.

If the customer wants something specific done, find out exactly what it is they want. Confirm this with them to be sure you understand what it is they want.

Step Seven - Explain What You CAN DO

Next, explain to the customer what you **can do**. If what the customer wants done is something you can do, **take action right away**. If what the customer wants done is something that you are unable to do, then you need to go on to the next step.

Step Eight - Discuss Alternatives and Agree On Action

You should fully discuss the alternative courses of action that might be taken regarding the customer's complaint and request for action. Present this in terms of benefits or drawbacks for the customer for each alternative. For instance, one alternative might be less costly to the customer, but might take more time, etc.

If none of the alternatives is satisfactory to the customer, and if you really can do nothing more for them, then get a person of higher responsibility and authority in your organization involved. (See the material on referring complaints upward located at the end of this section.)

Once the alternatives have been fully discussed, you and your customer need to **agree on a course of action**. Be as specific as possible. Be sure the customer knows **who** will do **what** and by

when, **where** and **how**, etc. This helps give customers confidence that something will really be done, and you are not just giving them the brush-off.

Step Nine - Take Action IMMEDIATELY

Once something has been agreed upon, you must take action **immediately** and implement the agreed upon solution. If there are any delays or deviations from the course of action agreed on, you must notify your customer immediately and negotiate a new plan of action. Remember, act **immediately** and **keep your promises** to the customer.

Step Ten - Follow Up to Ensure Customer Satisfaction

After the complaint has been resolved, you must try to follow up and contact the customer to make sure the solution to the problem was satisfactory to them. You should also take this opportunity to thank the customer for their continued business. Express your appreciation for their complaint and the opportunity it gave your organization to correct the situation. You can also say something like, "We have identified the cause(s) of the problem and are taking action to correct it. In the future, if you are not completely satisfied with our service, will you please let us know?"

Remember, in handling complaints and potentially explosive situations where customers might be lost, your conversations and handling of the complaint should be carefully documented. If necessary, report the situation to your manager. You should also record the information and maintain a file of customer complaints.

Referring Complaints Upward

Whenever possible, you should try to resolve complaints yourself. And, you should never refuse to help customers take their complaints higher up within your organization.

You need to have a clear understanding of what type of complaint you are able to handle, and which you are to refer to someone else. You also need to have a clear idea of how much authority you have in resolving complaints. When you are going to refer a complaint to your manager, follow these steps:

1. Have all the facts and information about the problem on hand. All of this data should be confirmed by the customer as being correct.

2. You should have a clear idea of what the customer wants and what they are asking be done about the problem.

3. You should also be ready to give an account of your conversation with the customer and tell your manager what you said to the customer. Explain the alternatives you offered and the customer's reactions to them. You must be honest and accurate and not distort the facts of the situation to make yourself look good in the eyes of your manager. If you try to fake it, you may make the situation worse.

4. Next, make sure you inform your manager of any promises you made to your customer. You should also be ready to recommend to your manager what you feel should be done now.

5. Lastly, you should come away from your meeting with your manager with a clear idea of what your role is going to be from this point on. Are you going to keep working on the problem or turn it over to your manager entirely? If you are to turn it over entirely, agree with your manager as to when and how you will be told about the final outcome.

If the customer asks you immediately to deal with your manager, ask for a chance to help them first. Then **promise** the customer if you don't handle the situation to their satisfaction, you personally will make sure they get a chance to talk to your manager.

The 10-Step Method In Action

To help you better understand these ten steps in action, look over this example of a real life situation. The customer, Dick Loper (Cust) had brought his new car in for service twice before. The problem with the car still exists. He is now bringing it in for a third time and meets with Mike Fisher (SG), the service-giver who is the auto dealer's service manager.

This case is abbreviated, but you'll be able to follow each of the steps in action.

Step One - Listen Without Interrupting

Cust: "You're the guy I'm looking for. I've brought my car in here twice now, and I've spent almost a hundred dollars and I still have the problem I came in here with! I've been inconvenienced twice now, once for a whole day and not a damn thing was done to the car! I was told you people had a decent service department, but you sure have to prove that to me! This kind of lousy service is terrible and your people have been no help whatsoever!"

SG: "Mr. Loper, I can see you are upset, and I would like to help with the problem."

Cust: "Well, I should hope so. This kind of run-around is no way to treat a customer!"

Step Two - Don't Get Defensive

Mike doesn't argue with the customer and say things like, "We don't give people the run-around," or "I have well-trained people, and I know they tried to help you." He listens carefully to what the customer has to say.

Step Three - Respond with GLAD • SURE • SORRY

SG: "Mr. Loper, I am **glad** that you are giving us another chance to work with you. I'm **sure** we can work this out to your satisfaction. However, I'm **sorry** there is a problem and you are upset about the way we've handled you."

Cust: "Well, I hope so."

Step Four - Express Empathy

SG: "We don't like to disappoint any of our customers. And I can understand how disappointed and upset you are at having to bring your car in two times and still not have the problem taken care of."

Cust: "Well, I'm glad you appreciate my situation. But what are you going to do about it?"

SG: "I promise that we are going to work out the problem to your satisfaction."

Step Five - Ask Questions to Understand the Problem

SG: "To make sure I understand the problem fully, may I ask you a few questions?"

Cust: "Sure, okay. Shoot."

SG: "When you brought the car in the first time, what was it for?"

Cust: "There was a shimmy or wobble in the car when I got it up to around 45 mph."

SG: "And did you have anything else done at that time?"

Cust: "Yes, a couple of things. There was a light out in the trunk. I had them fix the air conditioner ... and something else."

SG: "And those things were taken care of properly?"

Cust: "Yes, but not the wobble, that was the main reason I brought the car in."

SG: "I see here we put in new shocks and aligned the front end."

Cust: "That's right."

SG: "And that didn't solve the problem?"

Cust: "No, and I don't know why your man didn't roadtest the car, they could have found that out themselves. Your people were just guessing, and they guessed wrong."

SG: "You drove the car after your first visit and you had the exact same problem."

Cust: "No, it was a little better. But there was still a wobble or shimmy when I got the car up to 45. There still is."

SG: "So you brought it back (looking at records) two days later?"

Cust: "Right."

SG: "And what happened?"

Cust: "Nothing. You people kept the car the whole day. When I came in to pick up the car there was no one here to talk to. I assumed it was fixed. There was no charge, but as soon as I drove it, I felt the same thing. Nothing had been done on it, and you kept it a whole day."

79

SG: "I can see where that would be upsetting to you, and I'll find out why that happened, and fix it."

Step Six - Find Out What the Customer Wants

SG: "Let me be sure I have all the facts, okay Mr. Loper? You brought the car in the first time, mostly because of the shimmy at 45 mph. You had some other work done, and that was okay, but the shimmy was only slightly improved after we replaced the shock absorbers and aligned the front end. When you brought the car back a second time, we kept it for a day but apparently didn't work on it, and you still have the problem, right?"

Cust: "You got it."

SG: "Mr. Loper, I understand the situation. Obviously you want the cause of the shimmy found and fixed once and for all. We will do that. Is there anything else you want us to do?"

Cust: "Well, I want my money back. I paid for work that wasn't done. And I want you to fix the problem. And furthermore, I don't want to be inconvenienced by bringing the car back and forth, I want you to come and get it and then bring it back to me fixed!"

Step Seven - Explain What You CAN DO

SG: "Mr. Loper, I guarantee you we won't ask you to be inconvenienced by bringing your car back and forth. I can have someone come and get the car, and we will deliver it back to your house. We will take the car and roadtest it again and work on it until it is free of any problems."

Cust: "Okay! That sounds good, but I want my money back and I don't want to be charged for any additional work on my car!

Step Eight - Discuss Alternatives and Agree on Action

SG: "I understand you want your money back and don't want to pay any additional charges.

This is what I **can do** now. If you have the time, I will have one of my people roadtest the car with you. Then we will bring it into the shop and identify the problem and solve it while you wait.

Or, you could leave the car. I'll have someone drive you home. We'll check it out thoroughly, and I'll call you just as soon as we have a solution. I will also tell you exactly when we'll have it fixed for you.

If it is something that will take more time, I will arrange a loaner car for you. In any case, we will bring the car to your house when it is fixed. We will do whichever you prefer.

As to your request for your money back and further charges, I believe it is fair to charge you for the work that we completed to your satisfaction. That was the trunk light and the air conditioning. If we find the new shocks and/or alignment, which is normally the solution for a shimmy, were not necessary, we will refund your money. I will also guarantee that unless the necessary repair work is really major, you will not be charged for any further work connected with fixing the shimmy.

Will that work for you?"

Cust: "Okay, I'm happy with that.

I've got the time now and I would like to ride with whoever is going to roadtest the car. But then I'll leave the car and use your loaner until you get it fixed properly."

SG: "Fine, I'll get someone to roadtest the car with you now and arrange for a loaner car. I will call you with our results. How does that sound to you?"

Cust: "Excellent."

81

Step Nine - Take Action IMMEDIATELY

In this case, Mike Fisher, the Service Manager, discovered it was a faulty tire causing the problem. He called Mr. Loper. He asked Mr. Loper for his permission to replace the tire at 10% above cost and offered him free wheel-balancing. He also said he would refund the money charged for the new shock absorbers and front-end alignment. Mr. Loper agreed. Then, Mike Fisher arranged a time for the service technician to drive the car to Mr. Loper's house and roadtest the car with him for his final approval.

When the service technician returned to the dealership, he told Mike Fisher that Mr. Loper was totally satisfied that the shimmy had been corrected and the bill adjusted properly.

Step Ten - Follow Up to Ensure Customer Satisfaction

The next day, Mike Fisher called Mr. Loper to see if he was still satisfied. He again expressed his appreciation to Mr. Loper for bringing his complaint to him personally. He apologized for the difficulties. He briefly explained to Mr. Loper how he counseled the service technician and workshop manager and that he scheduled the technician for additional training. He also discussed the improvements he made in workshop procedures to ensure a higher level of quality service. Finally, he said how much he valued Mr. Loper's business and wanted him to return to his dealership.

Handling Complaints and Angry Customers

Complaints are valuable to service organizations, they are opportunities to retain customers and improve service. You should not be embarrassed about complaints, be afraid of them or get defensive with customers who complain. This will make you less effective in dealing with your customers. Try to see complaints as having a value.

Customers often have negative attitudes about complaints because they:

- May be embarrassed to confront you or your organization
- Are upset with the extra time and effort they have to spend to solve a problem
- Are angry about the extra expense or inconvenience they have experienced

Many customers don't complain, they just take their business elsewhere. Other customers are somewhat shy about complaining and can only do so if they have worked themselves up to a high level of anger and frustration. Some customers, fearful that nothing will be done about their complaint, kick up a big fuss, and rant and rave to make sure they receive attention and that something will be done about their complaint.

10-Step Method for Handling Complaints

Using this method increases your confidence in handling complaints. It also improves your ability to keep, not lose customers when handling complaints. It allows you to approach complaints with a consistently effective technique.

The 10 steps are:

1. Listen without interrupting
2. Don't get defensive
3. Respond with **GLAD** • **SURE** • **SORRY**
4. Express empathy

5. Ask questions to understand the problem
6. Find out what the customer wants
7. Explain what you **CAN DO**
8. Discuss alternatives and agree on action
9. Take action **IMMEDIATELY**
10. Follow up to ensure customer satisfaction

Remember to document complaints. Maintain a file of customer complaints. Try to handle complaints yourself, but never refuse to assist customers in taking their complaints to those with higher levels of authority in your organization. Be sure you have a clear idea of your authority and how far you can go in dealing with customer complaints.

Referring Complaints Upward To Your Manager

* Have all the information and facts
* Have a clear idea of what the customer wants
* Give a complete account of your conversation with your customer in trying to handle their complaint. Identify the alternatives you offered your customer and their reaction to each
* Discuss any promises you made and what you feel should be done now
* Get agreement on what your role will be regarding this complaint

Remember, if a customer immediately demands to deal with your manager, ask if you can have a chance to help first. Then promise your customer if you are unable to handle the matter to their satisfaction, you'll see to it they will get to see your manager.

9. Telephone Techniques

Much of today's service-giving is conducted by telephone. With the increased use of credit cards and the rapid development of telephonic and computer technology, you may find your major contact with customers is by telephone.

As a service-giver, you will find that you can use all of the quality service techniques in this book in working with customers by telephone. The basic skills of courtesy and communications (with the exception of body language) and the two major techniques, the 7-step method for giving quality service and the 10-step method for handling complaints, can be used to good advantage.

But in using the telephone, you have to be aware of some unique differences between telephone and face-to-face contacts with a customer. And, you have to know and use the appropriate telephone skills.

Here are some of the unique characteristics of the telephone in quality service-giving:

1. **Time distortion.** For most people a few seconds on the telephone seems like many minutes. This is partly because a customer who is asked to wait, or who experiences a brief delay, has nothing to do during that time. They get impatient much more quickly than they might otherwise. It is also due to people's expectation that telephones should work "instantly." Any delay or waiting is, therefore, unexpected and frustrating.

   A customer who might visit someone in person unexpectedly would be quite willing to wait a few minutes before being able to see the person. They realize they weren't expected, and the person they want to see may be occupied for a few minutes. But when calling by phone, the tolerance for time is greatly shortened, and a customer's view of how long things should take, and how long they actually take, is greatly distorted.

2. **Alienation and distance.** Telephone communications also have a dimension of apparent distance to them. There is a

high potential for making customers feel alienated and "left out" during delays and waiting times. It is to overcome this phenomenon that some organizations now play music when callers are put on hold or asked to wait. Supposedly the music is to comfort the caller and make them feel less "left out." You need to be aware of this alienation potential among customers and do everything you can to make a call warmer and more personal for your customer, especially if you have to make them wait.

3. **Lack of visual contact.** Since two people are unable to see each other during a phone call, you need to compensate for this. Tell customers what you are going to do for them. Keep customers informed of actions you are taking on their behalf. If the transaction were face-to-face, the customer could see what is happening. When the transaction is taking place by phone, you need to tell customers what is happening.

    This is especially true if you must leave the phone for a period of time as part of the service transaction. Don't just say to the customer something like, "Just a minute," and leave them waiting on the phone. Instead, explain your intentions, say, "I'm going to do such-and-such now, and I'll be back to you in about two minutes."

4. **Speed and action.** We tend to associate the telephone with speed and fast action. When the phone rings it may sound like a starting bell. You may be tempted to snatch the phone, start talking fast and almost get stampeded by a simple call.

    You would do better to stay calm as you prepare to use the telephone. It is helpful if you take a few seconds to compose yourself so you can make a transition from what you were doing just prior to the call. This will give you time to put a smile in your voice and answer the phone properly with a friendly, courteous greeting.

5. **Importance and urgency.** Closely associated with the idea of speed and the use of the telephone, is the idea of importance and urgency. Historically, the telephone was used only for very important and urgent calls. Today, calls that are quite

casual and routine still seem to take on an air of urgent importance. The ringing of the telephone always seems to be an urgent signal. Perhaps you, yourself, have been giving service in person to a customer and have allowed yourself to be interrupted by the ringing of the telephone. You must learn to take the call, but then inform the caller, "I am busy with another customer now, but I'll be with you in a few moments." But instead of doing this, the tyranny of the urgency associated with the telephone is such that service-givers often take the call but allow the telephone interruption to continue. Of course, this frustrates the customer they were serving in person.

A calmer, more rational approach to calls is needed. You must put them in the proper place in your service-giving so you are not stampeded by the "urgency" of phone calls.

6. **Interruption.** Every phone call is an interruption for the person being called. Telephone calls have a high potential for causing stress since they are always an interruption. If you use the telephone in your job, you need to adjust your attitude. Accept telephone calls as interruptions, but understand that these calls are an essential part of your job.

   Another problem with interruptions is the apparent assumption many customers make, that the person they are calling is immediately ready to respond to the call. They assume you were doing nothing that was as important as their call. This sort of arrogance can be particularly trying if you are the person being called. But since the customer has no way of knowing if they are interrupting, it's up to you to let them know. If you can take the call immediately, do so. If not, explain this to your customer and put them on hold or call them back later.

7. **Courtesy.** Because there is such an emphasis on speed and urgency, courtesy is often overlooked in using the phone. The attitude of some service-givers seems to be, if they are fast and effective in getting information across on the telephone, they are excused from having to observe the normal rules of courteous telephone manners. Nothing could be further from the truth.

The problem is made worse by the fact that without personal face-to-face contact, courteous behavior is not visible and you can only use courtesy words and phrases. Telephone calls without even this verbal courtesy will likely be highly frustrating for the customer and make them angry. You need to remember courtesy is even more important on the telephone than in person.

8. **Anonymity.** With just a voice at the other end of a telephone conversation, identifying people is difficult. Customers like to know WHO they are talking to, what position the person holds in the organization, etc. For this reason, you must always be quick to identify yourself, your department and your ability to help the customer. As you identify yourself, customers are more apt to identify themselves, thus making your telephone transactions more efficient and effective.

9. **Telephone skills.** By the time most people are six or seven years old, they have usually learned how the telephone works. But many people never progress beyond that early stage of telephone skill. Quality service-giving on the telephone requires familiarity with more refined skills and the knowledge of what to say, how to say it and when. You'll find many of these special telephone skills explained on the following pages.

10. **Telephone management.** With the increase in more sophisticated use of the telephone has come the need to pay closer attention to telephone management. The location and number of phones, kinds of equipment, location of supporting furniture and equipment, telephone message forms, telephone systems and procedures - all these need be worked out carefully. This will help ensure there is a consistent and efficient approach in your office to utilizing the telephone. This also includes the use of a list of frequently-called numbers, directories, and the ready availability of information that is needed in answering customer calls.

11. **Need for confirmation.** Again, because of the unique voice-only characteristic of telephone calls, the possibilities for mistakes, errors and misunderstandings are greater when using the telephone in service-giving. For this reason you

need to develop the skill of repeating information to get confirmation, asking for confirmation, asking for spelling and clarification where there seems to be confusion, etc. It is also helpful for you to develop the habit of keeping written records of your conversations and noting critical data. This can help facilitate later confirmation of what was actually said.

Some Telephone Skills

Below are a series of suggested telephone skills. Different organizations may have different policies and different approaches to these skills. Some organizations, for instance, may have more sophisticated message recording devices that make the old pencil and message pad obsolete.

The important thing for you as a service-giver is to find out the "correct" way to handle these telephone skills in your own organization. Then follow that method. If there are no "rules or procedures" that have been worked out as standard practice, then develop your own from the ideas on the following pages. As you think about your use of the telephone, review the material in the communications section of this book on talking and listening.

Your Telephone Voice

Speak at the right volume, not too loud or too soft. Try to have a smile in your voice, use a pleasant, friendly tone. Speak clearly, pronounce your words carefully. If you have an accent customers might not be able to understand, spell things out to make sure they have it right. Talk at the right speed, not too fast or too slow.

Be a Good Listener

Never interrupt, wait to be sure your caller is finished before you start to talk. Don't hesitate to ask your customer to repeat anything you don't understand. Repeat important information you are given such as numbers, spelling of words, important names of cities and streets. Listen for the caller's mood, try to determine not only what they are saying, but how they feel about it.

Answering a Call

Try to answer by the third ring. Remain calm. Take a moment to compose yourself before answering. To properly answer a call, do four things: (1) identify your organization (2) identify your department (3) identify yourself and (4) offer to help the caller.

Example: "Barrett and Barrett, Purchasing. This is Alice Markham, how may I help you?"

(The above statement would take three seconds to make.) Be ready with a message pad and pencil and listen carefully right from the beginning of the call.

If you are answering someone else's phone, you need to say something like -

"Barrett and Barrett, Alice Markham's phone. This is Bob Wilson, how may I help you?"

If you are going to be taking a message, always identify yourself. If the message is complicated, you may want to reassure the customer by saying something like, "My name is Bob Wilson, I work with Alice, and I'll see she gets the message right away."

Transferring a Call

If you are going to transfer a call, first of all, tell the customer what you are going to do. Warn them of any problems you might anticipate in the transfer. For instance, you might say, "I am going to transfer your call to Al Malloy in Shipping. They are sometimes away from the phone and it may take them a while to answer, please let it ring at least 10 times." Or, you might say, "I'm going to have to signal the switchboard and sometimes that may cause a break-off in the connection. If you do get cut off, the number in the department you want is extension 456."

The idea is to let the customer know what you are doing, and how the transfer will be handled. Of course, whenever possible, try to handle the call yourself and make it easy for your customer.

Placing a Call

Keep a directory of frequently called numbers handy. Remember time differences when you are calling long distance. On long distance calls, tell the answering party you are calling long distance. Be ready to talk, have all the necessary information right at hand. Allow the answering party enough time to answer, at least seven rings. When your call is answered, start by identifying yourself and your organization and the purpose of your call. If the answering party does not give their name, ask who it is you are talking with or give the name of the person with whom you wish to talk.

Asking a Caller to Hold

Tell the customer what you plan to do and about how long it will take. Ask them if they want to wait or have you call them back.

If you have to put someone on hold immediately, without being able to talk with them, check with them every 30 seconds to give them a progress report on the status of their call. If you think the time they will have to wait will be longer than three minutes, arrange to call them back. Try not to keep a customer waiting any longer than three minutes on the telephone, even when you are giving them progress reports, unless a longer wait is okay with them.

If there are long delays, thank the caller for being patient and waiting so long.

Taking a Telephone Message

Be prepared with a pencil and standardized message forms. Make sure your message includes the following: date of the call, time of the call, name of the person who was called, name of the person who made the call and their telephone number, organization and job title and a "preferred time" to call back. Include your name on message. Be sure you read the message and all information back to the caller. Get their confirmation it is correct before you hang up the phone.

Don't hesitate to have the caller spell out names and details you don't understand. Be sure you get the information correct.

Tell the caller, if you can, when the person will get the message. Deliver the message as soon as possible. Keep your promises to the caller.

Leaving a Telephone Message

When you leave a telephone message, give your name, your organization, and your telephone number. Tell the person who is taking your message when you will be available for call back. Explain in the message the purpose for your call. Give the called person details if possible, so when they call you back, they are prepared with the proper information. I suggest that you say: **"For my own peace of mind, would you please read that back to me?"** Asking in this polite way encourages the message-taker to repeat your message, giving you confidence that all the details are correct. Ask for their name, too, so you will know who handled your message. Ask when the message is expected to be delivered.

Closing a Call

If necessary, summarize the substance of your call confirming details discussed or follow-up actions promised. Besides just saying "goodbye," try to close with a friendly, courteous closing such as:

"Is there anything else I can do for you?"
"It was nice talking to you."
"Please call again if I can be of help in the future."
"Thank you for calling."
"Thanks for your help."
"We appreciate your business, Mr. Johnson."

Remembering and using these telephone techniques will enable you to give the same quality service to your customers on the telephone as you would give them in person.

Telephone Techniques

Much of today's service-giving is conducted on the telephone. You can use communications and courtesy skills, the 7-step method for giving quality service and the 10-step method for handling complaints while using the phone, as well as in face-to-face situations. There are some unique characteristics of the telephone in service-giving:

* Time distortion
* Alienation and distance
* Lack of visual contact
* Speed and action
* Importance and urgency
* Interruptions
* Courtesy
* Anonymity
* Telephone skills
* Telephone management
* Need for confirmation

The essential telephone techniques are:

* Using the right voice
* Being a good listener
* Answering a call
* Transferring a call
* Placing a call
* Asking a caller to hold
* Taking a message
* Leaving a message
* Closing a call

10. Coping With Job Stress

Every job produces stress. Some stress is good, it motivates us to act, to respond and get things done. Too much of it, however, becomes "negative" stress. According to the American Institute of Stress, this kind of negative stress costs American business and industry nearly 75 billion dollars a year through employee sickness and injuries.

You, as a service-giver, have a job that is more likely to produce negative stress according to the National Institute for Occupational Safety and Health. For this reason, you need to be aware of stress, the harmful effects it can cause and how you can cope with it. Being able to handle stress means you'll be a more effective quality service-giver.

What is Stress?

Stress is your chemical, emotional and psychological reaction to the events going on around you. When something happens, you respond. Positive stress moves you to act, to respond and deal with the events around you in a useful, productive way. Negative stress is an excessive build-up of stress and occurs when you experience a great deal of stress over a long period of time with no relief. Negative stress can cause you to perform poorly on the job and can have several harmful effects, among them:

Physical Harm -   Research shows that negative stress over a period of time can help induce heart attacks, ulcers, diabetes, colitis, cancer, arthritis, backaches, and can increase your chance of accidents and infections.

Emotional Harm -   Negative stress can wear away your emotional strength and leave you emotionally unstable, subject to unusually strong expressions of your feelings at the wrong time and place. For instance, you might burst into tears or get extremely angry at some minor incident.

Psychological Harm - Experience with negative stress also shows it can lead you to lose your rational powers and ability to think straight. You find it hard to plan, make decisions and solve problems, and you may start to act in irrational, non-productive ways. You may make frequent errors and mistakes.

Sources of Negative Stress

There are three primary sources of negative stress. Stress from each of these areas is not inevitable, although each of them can produce negative stress.

Job Environment

Some of the potential negative stress producers in your job environment might be:

1. Light
2. Noise
3. Tobacco smoke
4. Disorganization (things in a helter-skelter mess)
5. Unsanitary conditions
6. Unsafe conditions
7. Unhealthy climate (temperature, humidity, ventilation)
8. Lack of supplies when needed
9. Faulty or inadequate equipment
10. Uncomfortable furniture
11. Poor work situation layout

Job Activities

Some of the potential negative stress producers in your job activities might be:

1. Lack of opportunity for you to participate in decision-making and planning in your job area
2. Interruptions
3. Frequent, rapid and sudden changes
4. Unrealistic time demands on you
5. Peer relationships

6. Confusion over your responsibilities and authority
7. Relationship with manager
8. Excessive amount of work
9. Errors and mistakes you make
10. Customer contacts that are mostly negative
11. Constant flow of complex problems and crises in your job
12. Your lack of job skills

Your Personality

Research shows the following personality traits identify people who are prone to suffer the harmful effects of negative stress:

1. High need to control everything, to always "win"
2. Tendency to be a perfectionist, intolerance of errors or mistakes
3. Impatient, ALWAYS in a hurry
4. Must do several things at once
5. High need for approval and recognition
6. Guilt feelings when doing "nothing"

What Causes Negative Stress?

There are two primary causes of negative stress, and both are things you can do something about. The first cause is **perception,** how you interpret what is happening around you and how you feel about it. Your reactions to events and circumstances will be stressful or not depending on how you look at them.

For example, your managers may not speak to you in the morning when they come in. You may interpret this as meaning you are in their disfavor, maybe they are even ready to fire you. You start to worry and grow fearful or get angry at having been deliberately slighted. Later you may discover it was a plain and simple over-sight. Your manager's failing to say good morning didn't produce the negative stress. Your **perception** of what that meant was the culprit.

The point is you react based on what you **think** is happening. You get angry, or fearful and develop negative stress, depending on your **perception**. Keep in mind, events themselves do not cause stress, your interpretation of them is the real problem.

A second cause of negative stress is your **expectations**, what you think **should** or **ought** to happen. For instance, you may expect your customers to know certain procedures, how to fill out certain forms, etc. If they approach you without the correct form properly filled out, you may be frustrated and angry. You'll be saying to yourself, "Stupid people, they **OUGHT** to know what is required, they **SHOULD** fill out the proper form first." But if you do not **expect** customers will know how to fill out the form, you won't be upset. The not-filling-out-the-form-properly doesn't cause the stress, it is your **expectation**, your use of "oughts" and "shoulds" that gets you into trouble.

How to Cope with Negative Stress

There are several techniques you can use to reduce negative stress on the job and avoid its harmful emotional, psychological and physical effects. There are also "buffer" activities you can pursue **off** the job to help you cope with negative job stress.

1. Quality Service Techniques

By using the techniques outlined in this book, you can do a lot to help avoid negative stress. They are designed to make service-giving less stressful and more rewarding and satisfying. These techniques are helpful to you in coping with those highly stressful contacts involving angry customers, complaints and problems.

2. Change Perceptions

Think through the way you are approaching your job and your organization. Do you have a clear perception of what's really happening and why? If not, check with your manager. Talk to customers and other service-givers. Be sure you are developing a clear and positive perception of what's going on around you.

One bank employee just hated busy Fridays. Her perception of them was almost totally negative. She usually performed poorly on that day and had a miserable time each week. She helped herself cope with her job stress by thinking things through. She began to say to herself, "Friday is the best day of the week for most customers to bank. I should be glad we are so busy and so many customers come in then. Friday is a big volume day for the organization. Instead of complaining, I should be grateful each week we have a Friday!"

She began to accept Fridays as a particularly challenging day of the week. Eventually, she was able to develop a much more positive attitude toward her job and her customers. She started to reduce her negative job stress by changing the way she thought about Fridays.

3. Change Expectations

"People **shouldn't** complain." "People **ought** to be on time for their appointments." "People **should** expect to wait a while before I get to them." These kinds of **"oughts"** and **"shoulds"** reflect your expectations. Since most of the time other people fail to meet your expectations, this can cause you to be frustrated and angry and develop negative job stress.

The trick is to change your expectations. If you expect some customers **will** complain, if you realize complaints are good ways for you to **improve** your service; if you expect people **will** sometimes be late for appointments; that some customers **will** be unhappy if they have to wait; then when those things do happen, you will be able to handle them much more easily. You will be less frustrated and angry and suffer much less negative job stress.

Consider this. A librarian I knew had very unrealistic expectations of the children that used the library. She was constantly upset. The children were noisy, messy and failed to obey all the rules and regulations she had established. She expected them to be perfect in their behavior at all times and was constantly frustrated and disappointed that they were not.

One day, she was so frustrated she blurted out, "If it wasn't for these darned kids, we could have a really nice library!" When she heard herself say that, she was shocked. Without the children, there would be no children's library. And without a children's library, she wouldn't have a job. Some of the other librarians laughed at her comment. Then she did, too. She realized her expectations had become so unreal they were causing her a great deal of misery and negative job stress. She toned down her expectations and made them more realistic. After that she began to enjoy the children more and found her days at work were not so stressful.

Check out your own expectations. Are you using too many "oughts" and "shoulds" in your thinking? If so, re-thinking these expectations may help you reduce your own job stress.

4. Relieve Stress Build-Up

There are three kinds of "buffer" activities you can pursue to relieve negative stress that builds up on the job:

a. Exercise - Swimming, biking, running and walking are among the best kinds of exercise. Any regular, physical activity is usually good for helping relieve the tensions of negative stress.

b. Do something different - After work, find a leisure time activity that is dramatically different from what you do on the job. Doing something quite different helps you get a fresh perspective on things and relieves stress build-up.

c. Talk with others - Another way to relieve stress build-up is by talking it out with others. Be sure it is with someone who is understanding and is willing to listen!

5. Develop a Less Stressful Lifestyle

If both your job and your lifestyle away from work are stress producing, it will be hard for you to avoid negative stress build-up. If you find it difficult to control stress at work, you can at least reduce negative stress in your off-work hours by:

a. Not smoking   d. Getting sufficient sleep
b. Drinking in moderation   e. Developing leisure-time activities
c. Following a proper diet   f. Exercising

As a service-giver you have a job that offers many benefits and satisfactions. But your job also has a high potential for negative stress. Since you have to be on your best behavior at all times, and because you have to deal with people under all sorts of circumstances (some of them unpleasant), the potential for stress is there.

Your single, best reason for increasing your use of the quality service-giving skills outlined in this book is that it will help you reduce negative stress in your job. I believe you can be a happier, more satisfied person and perform your job more effectively as a service-giver if you are free of negative job stress.

Coping With Job Stress

Every job produces stress. "Positive" stress motivates us to respond, to take action and get things done. Too much stress becomes "Negative" and can be harmful. It is estimated that negative stress costs the United States nearly 75 billion dollars a year in related sickness and injury. Service-giving jobs are prone to be particularly stressful.

Stress is your body's chemical, emotional and psychological response to what is going on around you. Negative stress can have three harmful effects: physical, emotional and psychological. The three primary sources of "negative" stress are:

- * Job environment
- * Job activities
- * Your personality

There are two primary causes of "negative" stress:

- * Perception - how you see, interpret and react to what you think is going on around you
- * Expectations - what you feel **should** or **ought** to happen

Five Things You Can Do To Cope With "Negative" Stress

1. - Use quality service-giving techniques consistently
2. Change erroneous perceptions
3. Develop more realistic expectations
4. Relieve stress build-up by:
    - -exercising
    - -doing something different
    - -talking with others
5. Develop a less stressful lifestyle:
    - -stop smoking
    - -drink only in moderation
    - -follow a proper diet
    - -get sufficient sleep
    - -develop leisure time activities
    - -exercise regularly

11. What's Next?
Now that you have learned these quality service skills and techniques, here are a few pointers for continuing your learning, and for putting what you have learned into action.

1. **Read.** Use this book as a study guide. Pick out the parts you feel would be most helpful to you in your particular job. Read these parts over carefully. Read other things about the same topic. For instance, if the material on using the telephone is the most useful to you, find other books and pamphlets on using the telephone effectively, and read them.

2. **Plan.** Sit down and develop a plan of action. Set some goals for yourself. Applying what you have learned in this book won't happen automatically, you have to work at it. That means developing a plan, then putting it into action. Try to set deadlines for yourself. Pick a date when you feel a particular improvement in your service-giving will have been accomplished. Write out your plan and the different things you are going to do to make it happen on schedule.

3. **Start.** Pick one or two things you want to work on. Then start, do something. Don't try to apply all the things you learned in this book at once. Take it one step at a time. But as soon as you can, start! Once you get underway, the rest will be easy.

4. **Journal.** From now on, keep a little notebook in which you write your service-giving experiences. Keep track of unusual events and how you handled them. Include both good and bad experiences. Make notes on what you did and what you **might** have done after you have had a chance to think about it. Every so often, review your notebook. Use it as a sort of progress report on your success in developing improved quality service-giving techniques. Try to make entries in it daily, and review it about every two weeks.

5. **Other service-givers.** Talk to other service-givers with whom you work. Get their ideas on using quality service techniques. If they haven't read the book, tell them about it. Find out what they do with customers and why. Share your ideas with them. Working with other service-givers, you can learn to help each other by giving each other feedback. It may also lead to cooperation in standardizing the approach to serving customers in your office or place of work.

6. Your manager. Discuss the ideas in this book with your manager. Get their ideas. Get agreement on how the ideas in this book can be applied to your particular organization. If your manager disagrees with you, find out why and how you can adapt the ideas in the book to meet with your manager's approval. Determine their commitment to quality service. Try to reach agreement on your job authority and responsibilities in dealing with customers. What problems are you authorized to handle, and what problems need to go to your manager? Be sure you are clear on all policies, procedures and your job priorities. Don't be afraid to ask even if your manager doesn't seem too willing to talk about it. You will find it more difficult to give your customers true quality service if you and your manager are not in harmony.

7. Customers. One of the best places to get feedback on your success in using quality service techniques is your customers. Especially regular customers. Let them know what you are trying to do. Show them the book. Ask for their comments on your performance and, in general, how they feel about the service your organization gives them. When your customers **do** give you feedback, don't get defensive and argue with them or explain. Thank them for their comments and ask if there is anything else they would care to share with you. You might even want to consider a little survey, a form with questions your customers fill out about your service. Keep it short and simple. **Use** the information. Listen to what your customers say to you, and then act on that information.

8. Improve the system. Working with your manager and other service-givers in your organization, try to think of ways you can improve your operations. Look at the environment around you - are there better facilities, equipment, tools, materials, supplies you could use to improve service? Are there changes that could be made in the systems, policies and procedures in your organization that would improve your service to your customers? Are there ways you could help educate your customers so they know better how to approach and use the services of your organization?

Quality service consists of good service systems as well as proper service-giving techniques. Look for barriers to good service in your own work area. Change things or make suggestions for changes that will help you deliver an improved service to your customer.

By continuing to improve your use of the ideas and techniques contained in this book, you'll improve your skills as a professional quality service-giver. As that happens, you'll improve your job satisfaction, reduce job stress and enjoy the rewards of a really professional service-giver. Good luck!

ABOUT THE AUTHOR

Mary Gober is internationally-acclaimed as the most dynamic force in customer service culture development today. Her expertise and knowledge in the field are unrivalled!

For the past 24 years, in 27 countries, Mary Gober's seminars, coaching, books and videos, presenting her highly-successful 'GOBER METHOD'$_{TM}$ have given thousands of executives, managers and front-line staff the skills and strategies to achieve unprecedented levels of customer satisfaction and loyalty.

Mary Gober is the author of three books:

* The Art of Giving Quality Service
* Is Your Organization Customer-Focused? Assessment Audit
* Strategies for Building a Customer-Focused Organization

THE 'GOBER METHOD'$_{TM}$

Mary Gober developed the 'GOBER METHOD'$_{TM}$ to provide a strategic service culture framework for executives and managers, and a format for developing front-line service competencies.

It is a positive, proactive, inspirational process that elicits in all staff a sense of urgency and personal accountability for customer satisfaction, loyalty and business growth through increased sales and service.

The 'GOBER METHOD'$_{TM}$ encompasses 3 Aspects:

Aspect 1 - The Psychology of Service$_{TM}$ - The Service Excel Mind-Set$_{TM}$
The required attitude, values and philosophy for superior service performance.

Aspect 2 - The GOBER Language of Service$_{TM}$
A powerful and natural style of communication, adaptable to an individual's unique personality, that is proven to increase confidence and dramatically improve the quality of conversations and relationships.

Aspect 3 - The GOBER Management Framework$_{TM}$
An easy-to-implement management structure and set of how-to strategies for assessing and expanding a dynamic service culture.

104

INTERNATIONAL EXPERIENCE

Mary Gober has *personally* done consulting and training in these **24 countries** around the world:

North America

The United States
Canada

Australia & Asia

Australia
New Zealand
Hong Kong
Singapore
Malaysia

Europe & UK

Belgium
The Netherlands
France
Sweden
Norway
Estonia
Russia
England
Scotland
Ireland
Wales

Middle East

Saudi Arabia
Dubai
Qatar
Abu Dhabi

Africa

Egypt
South Africa

WORLDWIDE CLIENTS

Clients, *worldwide,* include:

Abu Dhabi Gas Industries
Airservices Australia
Alliance Textiles
American Trucking Association
ARAMCO (Arabian American Oil
   Company) Medical Services
Armaguard, Mayne Nickless
Australian Capital Territory
   (ACT) Chamber of Commerce
Australian Customer Service
   Association
Australian Parliament House
Australian Quality Council
Bankers Trust
Baring Asset Management
   (Member ING Group)
Bethesda Hospital
BHP Petroleum
Birmingham Midshires
   Building Society
Box Hill Institute of Technical
   and Further Education

BP Oil
British Airways
Building Service Contractors of
   New Zealand
Central Milton Keynes
   Shopping Centre
Centrelink
Chadwell Heath Care
   (Nursing) Home
Chameleon Training &
   Consulting Ltd.
Coca-Cola
Collins Radio Constructors,
   Rockwell International
Commonwealth Department of
   Health and Family Services
Commonwealth Office of
   Rehabilitation and
   Workman's Compensation
Concourse Cars
Conoco, DuPont
Consolidated Paper Industries

Crown Casino Ltd.
Customer Service Management
DeTeWe
Dubai Airport
Dubai Petroleum
Dun & Bradstreet Software
eCustomerServiceWorld
Eastman Chemical Company
Eastman Kodak Company
ElderWood Nursing Homes
Elgas Ltd.
Ericsson Australia & New
   Zealand
Family Housing Group
First National Bank of Chicago
Galileo Southern Cross
General Electric
  Electric Insurance
  Electric Mutual Liability
  Insurance
  GE Corporate Benefits Delivery
  GE Health & Disability Center
George Weston Foods Ltd.
Goldwell Cosmetics
Hazelwood Power Corporation
Help Desk Institute
Hilton International
Hilton Reserverations Worldwide
Honeywell Control Systems
Hunt Real Estate Corporation
I.I.R. Pty. Ltd.
Incitec
Kangan-Bateman Institute of
   Technical and Further
   Education
Kinetek Energy
Kodak Australasia
L & K: Rexona, Unilever
Laing Homes
Lend Lease Employer Systems

Lex Brooklands Volvo
   Concessionaires UK
Litigation Management, Inc.
London & Quadrant Housing
   Trust
Management Technology
   Education
Mattel
Mayne Nickless Ltd.
Mercedes-Benz
   UK Dealer Council
Mobil Oil
Monaco Motors
Mt. St. Mary's Hospital
National Australia Bank
National Australian University
New Rowley Motors
New Zealand Insurance
Novotel London West Hotel &
   Convention Centre
Occidental Chemical
Pacific Power
Paramount Cleaning Services
Paychex
PayConnect Solutions
QANTAS
Qatar General Petroleum
RCA
Research Machines (RM)
Riverside Press
Roswell Park Cancer Institute
Royal Bank of Scotland
Saudi ARAMCO
Scott Paper Company
Scuderia-Veloce Motors
Sedgwick James Claims
   Management Services
Sun Bank
Swinburne University
Telecom Australia (Telstra)

WORLDWIDE CLIENTS *continued ...*

The Human Resources Forum,
  Richmond Events
The Society of Consumer
  Affairs Professionals
Total Quality Management
  Institute - New Zealand
Touchpaper
Tourism Council Australia
Tower Homes
Triple M FM Radio
United Healthcare Corporation
Volvo Australia
Volvo Car Corporation
Waitrose Supermarkets
Wards Skyroad, Mayne Nickless
Water Corporation of Western
  Australia
WCA Hospital
Westar Gas
Western Melbourne Regional
  Economic Development
  Organization
Western New York
  Healthcare Association
Woolworths/Safeway
  Supermarkets
Xerox Corporation
Xerox Learning Systems
Yarra Valley Water Ltd.
Zurich Financial Services

PUBLIC OPEN SEMINARS

In addition to working with her private clients, Mary Gober has presented **PUBLIC OPEN SEMINARS** to *thousands* of participants in the major capital cities of *North America, Europe, Africa, Australia, Asia* and the *Middle East.* Participants have represented many of the world's largest and most successful companies.

These seminars have been on the topics of:

* **The 'GOBER METHOD'** ₜₘ
* **Building a Customer-Focused Organization**
* **The Art of Giving Quality Customer Service**
* **Leadership Skills**
* **Coaching and Counseling for Service Excellence**
* **Customer-Focused Selling**
* **Teambuilding**
* **World's Best Practice Telephone Techniques**
* **Critical Skills for Secretarial and Administrative Staff**

CONFERENCE SPEAKER

Mary Gober has been a *Keynote Speaker* and *Awards Presenter* at a number of prestigious Corporate and International Conferences focusing on **Customer Service, Leadership** and **Team Development**, including:

The 2003 North American Conference on Customer Management - *"The Psychology and Language of Stunning Customer Service"*

Orlando, Florida

The 2003 European Conference on Customer Management - *"Rejuvenating and Motivating a 'Burnt Out' Workforce"*

London, England

Central Milton Keynes Shopping Centre (thecentre:mk) Retailers Spring 2003 Event -
"The 'GOBER METHOD'ₜₘ – A Proven Strategy to Increase Sales, Improve Service and Motivate Your People"

Milton Keynes, England

The 2003 Senior Management Conference, Waitrose (Supermarkets) Ltd - Leading on Product and Service -
"Dominate the Competition with The 'GOBER METHOD'ₜₘ"

Newport Gwent, Wales

The 2002 Coca-Cola Management Conference, Towards World-Class Together -
"The Key to Becoming a World-Class Organization is YOU!"

Dublin, Ireland

The 2002 London & Quadrant Housing Trust Governing Board and Directors Conference -
"Creating Places Where People Want to Live with the 'GOBER METHOD'ₜₘ"

Windsor, England

Zurich Financial Services 2002 Management and Staff Conference - *"How to Raise the Bar and Deliver Consistent Customer Service"*

The Belfry, England

108

The 2002 DeTeWe and Mitel Networks Customer Conference at the Institute of Directors – Strengthening Professional Service Through Advanced Communication Technology -
"Developing People to Deliver World-Class Service"

London, England

Baring Asset Management – Member ING Group, 2002 Country Heads Conference, Managing Profitable Growth in a Tough Business Environment -
"What Makes a Client-Focused Organization?"

London, England

Laing Homes 2002 Management and Staff Conference -
"The Impact of the 'GOBER METHOD'$_{TM}$ in Laing Homes' Award-Winning Customer Service"

London, England

Touchpaper Customer Conference 2002, The New Face of IT –
"A Powerful Strategy for Motivating Your Team to Consistently Deliver Superior Service"

York, England

The 2002, Fifteenth Annual Conference for Help Desk and Support Professionals, Lip Service or Life Saver? –
"How To Achieve a Superior Service Style That Motivates Staff and Distinguishes Your Organization!"

London, England

The 2002 European Conference on Customer Management - *"A Powerful Strategy for Building a Customer-Centric Organization"*

London, England

The Society of Consumer Affairs Professionals (SOCAP) UK and Europe 2001 Conference - *"The 'GOBER METHOD'$_{TM}$ for the Strategy, Psychology & Language of Service$_{TM}$"*

London, England

The First European Human Resources Forum, 2001 - *"Creating a Totally Customer-Focused Culture"*
Aboard the COSTA ROMANTICA -
Amsterdam, The Netherlands

The 2001 European Conference on Customer Management - *"Putting the Customer at the Heart of Your Customer Contact Centre" and "The 'GOBER METHOD'*$_{TM}$ *- An Application Clinic"*
London, England

The 2000, Eighth Annual, Customer Service Management Conference, The Human Touch in a Digital World - *"Service Strategy With a Difference!"*
London, England

"An Audience with Mary Gober" presented by British Airways & Chameleon Training & Consulting Ltd.
London, England - March & August 2000

The 1999, Seventh Annual, Australian Customer Service National Summit Customer Service for the New Millenium - *"A Dynamic Approach to Customer Service"*
Melbourne, Victoria

The 1997 Australian Customer Service Association Conference - *"Customer Service - A Winning State"*
Perth, Western Australia

The 1997 Australian Customer Service State Awards
Perth, Western Australia

The 1997, Third Annual, Australian Customer Service National Summit - *"Will Australia Win a Gold Medal for Customer Service at the Sydney 2000 Olympics?"*
Sydney, New South Wales

The Chief Minister's 1997 ACT Customer Service Awards
Canberra, Australian Capital Territory (ACT)

The 1996, Second Annual, Australian Customer Service National Summit

Melbourne, Victoria

The 1996 Australian Customer Service National Awards

Melbourne, Victoria

The 1996, Fifth Annual, Tourism Council Australia Conference - Council of Australian Tourism Students

Perth, Western Australia

Western Melbourne Regional Economic Development Organization - *"Practical Tools for Building a World-Class, Customer-Focused Organization"*

Melbourne, Victoria - 1996

The 1993 Leadership Challenge - A Symposium for the Chief Executive - Australian Quality Council

Sanctuary Cove, Queensland

Managing the Quality Environment - An Invitation to Chief Executives - Total Quality Management Institute of New Zealand

Wellington, New Zealand, 1993

Quality - The Total Organization Strategy
Third International Conference - Total Quality Management Institute of New Zealand

Wellington, New Zealand, 1993

The First International Service and Quality Forum -
Lakewood Conferences - Euro Disney

Paris, France, 1992

Quality in the Community

Woollongong, New South Wales, 1992

Quality Through Customer-Driven Service

Hobart, Tasmania, 1992

BOOKS, ARTICLES, VIDEOS and COURSEWARE

In addition to **The Art of Giving Quality Service**, Mary Gober has written:

* **Strategies for Building a Customer-Focused Organization**

* **Is Your Organization Customer-Focused? Assessment Audit**

* Article – *"Mary Gober: A Life, A Method, A Mind-Set"* Training Journal, March 2002

* Article – *"Positivity vs. Negativity in the Workplace"* Customer Management, January–February 2003

* Article – *"The Office of Fair Trading, 'It's Your Call' 2003 Campaign – Help or Horror?"* Customer Management, March–April 2003

* Articles – See Mary Gober's regular column in each 2003 issue of Customer Management

* Video - *How to Deal With People Over the Telephone*

* Courseware - **CUSTOMER-FOCUS MODULE**, including *Student Guide and Instructor's Guide* for the **Diploma in Quality Management**, Australian Quality College, The Australian Quality Council

* Video & Courseware - *Custom Designed*, **Quality Service Training Program** - **LEADER'S GUIDE** and **PARTICIPANT'S WORKBOOK** for **VIDEO:** *"Awesome Service II - Moments of CARE"* Woolworths/Safeway Supermarkets, Australia, 1995

* Videos & Courseware - *Custom Designed*, **NEW STAFF INDUCTION VIDEO - *"Welcome to Woolworths"*** and **ALL STAFF VIDEO, *"Introduction to the Customer CARE Culture"*** with **LEADER'S GUIDES** and **PARTICIPANT'S WORKBOOKS** Woolworths/Safeway Supermarkets, Australia, 1998

BOOKS, ARTICLES, VIDEOS and COURSEWARE *continued ...*

* Videos & Courseware - **Custom Designed**, **TWO VIDEOS** - **"Delighting Customers"** and **"Confidence with Customers"** with **LEADER'S GUIDES** and **PARTICIPANT'S WORKBOOKS**
Woolworths/Safeway Supermarkets, Australia, 1999

'GOBER METHOD'_{TM} ASSOCIATE CONSULTANTS

Mary Gober has personally selected, trained and accredited a team of Associate Consultants to assist her in teaching and coaching the 'GOBER METHOD'_{TM} worldwide.

To date, Associate Consultants have delivered the 'GOBER METHOD'_{TM} in 12 countries:

Australia	Japan
Belgium	Mexico
England	Singapore
Scotland	Sweden
Estonia	The Netherlands
Cyprus	The United States

Clients include:

Alexander Forbes	Mattel
Asda	Nestlé Rowntree
Bristol City Council	Novotel London West Hotel and Convention Centre
Britannia Airways	Presentation Housing
Brooklyn Ford	Research Machines (RM)
Chadwell Heath Care Home	Reuters
DeTeWe	Sun Bank
Family Housing Group	thecentre:mk (Central Milton Keynes Shopping Centre)
Gojobsite	
Hilton Reservations Worldwide	The Law Society
House of Commons, British Parliament	Tower Homes
Laing Homes	Waitrose Supermarkets
London & Quadrant Housing Trust	Wesleyan Financial Services
	Zurich Financial Services

BEFORE ENTERING CONSULTING

Before establishing her own business in 1979, Mary Gober:

- held a faculty position in the School of Education at the **University of Illinois**. She was one of the *pioneers* in the research and development of Computer-Based Education.

- lived in **Saudi Arabia** and worked for the world's largest oil company, **ARAMCO (Arabian American Oil Company)**. She conducted seminars on Management and Interpersonal Skills to a widely-diverse group of people from *different* cultures, nationalities and religions.

EDUCATION

BS Degree, University of Kansas, 1971
MS Degree, University of Illinois, 1973

Training and Consulting Services

Mary Gober and her team of accredited 'GOBER METHOD'$_{TM}$ Associate Consultants *personally* assist organizations to **begin to implement** and/or **improve** their efforts at satisfying and retaining customers by enhancing their service ethic, delivery and processes.

'GOBER METHOD'$_{TM}$ 2-Day Seminar

After on-site research and orientation to the client's organization to understand and assess service culture and performance, the 2-Day Seminar is offered. It is entitled:

The 'GOBER METHOD' For the Strategy, Psychology & Language of Service$_{TM}$

The Seminar focuses, in depth, on Aspect 1 and Aspect 2 of the 'GOBER METHOD'$_{TM}$.

Aspect 1   **The Psychology of Service$_{TM}$ and The Service Excel Mind-Set$_{TM}$**

The required attitude, values and philosophy for superior service behavior and a consistent corporate service style.

Aspect 2   **The GOBER Language of Service$_{TM}$**

A powerful style of communication that is flexible to an individual's own character and personality. Ensures that service and sales conversations with clients and colleagues are managed competently in face-to-face and telephone situations, and in e-mail and written correspondence.

ON-THE-JOB COACHING

After the 'GOBER METHOD'$_{TM}$ 2-Day Seminar, Mary Gober and her Associate Consultants provide personal coaching to assist individuals and teams to implement and master the 'GOBER METHOD'$_{TM}$.

TRAIN-THE-COACH PROCESS

This is a process of training and coaching which enables and licenses a client's own managers and team leaders to conduct 'GOBER METHOD'$_{TM}$ coaching.

ADVANCED MARY GOBER SEMINARS

Advanced Skills Seminars build on the 'GOBER METHOD'$_{TM}$ 2-Day Training. Mary Gober presents the 'GOBER METHOD'$_{TM}$ approach in the following in-depth, specific seminars:

* Confidence & Composure Under Fire
* Listening - The Key to Effective Relationships
* Negotiation, Influencing, Selling and Persuasion Skills
* Be a Satisfied Customer - How to Get Quality Service, Everytime!
* Teamwork Skills for Service Excellence
* Customer-Focused Writing
* Receptionists - The First Point of Service Excellence

SERVICE LEADERSHIP TRAINING

Managers and team leaders learn how to take their service culture to a new level. Specific Seminar topics include:

* Modeling the exemplary service skills of the 'GOBER METHOD'$_{TM}$
* Demonstrating the 'GOBER METHOD' Mind-Set$_{TM}$ and speaking the GOBER Language of Service$_{TM}$
* Selecting, training, motivating and empowering service staff
* Building productive service teams
* Enhancing service-givers' self-esteem
* Providing effective coaching and counseling
* Implementing and measuring service standards

SERVICE CULTURE ASSESSMENT AND DEVELOPMENT USING THE GOBER MANAGEMENT FRAMEWORK~TM~

Based on the books, **Is Your Organization Customer-Focused? Assessment Audit** and **Strategies for Building a Customer-Focused Organization**, Mary Gober and her team of accredited Associate Consultants assist client teams to (1) understand her 12-Component Management Framework (Aspect 3 of the 'GOBER METHOD'~TM~) (2) complete and discuss the **Assessment Audit** questions and (3) develop and implement realistic **Strategies** and priority-based Action Plans for improvement.

Special Programs and consulting in the areas of:

* Developing Organization Strategy and Compelling Vision
* Researching Customer Needs
* Changing Organization Structure
* Improving Service-Delivery Processes
* Developing Leadership Skills
* Measuring Customer and Employee Satisfaction
* Setting Service Standards and Measuring Service Efficiency
* Establishing Complaint Handling Procedures and Measuring Systems
* Developing Organization Culture Change Agents
* Building and Developing Team Skills
* Strategies for Customer Education
* Improving Customer and Staff Environment
* Communication Strategies with Staff, Customers and Media

TEAMBUILDING PROGRAMS

Managers - skills in creating and leading teams that improve participation, service, quality and productivity.

Staff - interpersonal, problem-solving, decision-making and team leadership skills for successful group work.

TEAMBUILDING PROGRAMS *continued ...*

Group-to-Group -   a variety of interventions aimed at bringing distinct groups together to achieve different objectives such as: defining service and quality relationships, building partnerships and common focus, resolving conflicts, exploring new issues, building morale, improving processes and long-term planning.

For further information about 'GOBER METHOD'$_{TM}$ training and consulting services, and to order additional copies of this book, or Mary Gober's other books, **Is Your Organization Customer-Focused? Assessment Audit**, and **Strategies for Building a Customer-Focused Organization**, please contact:

Jane Burke,
Executive Assistant to Mary Gober
Mary Gober International

Email janeburke@marygober.com

Telephone +1 716 759 2847

Facsimile +1 716 759 8165

Website www.marygober.com